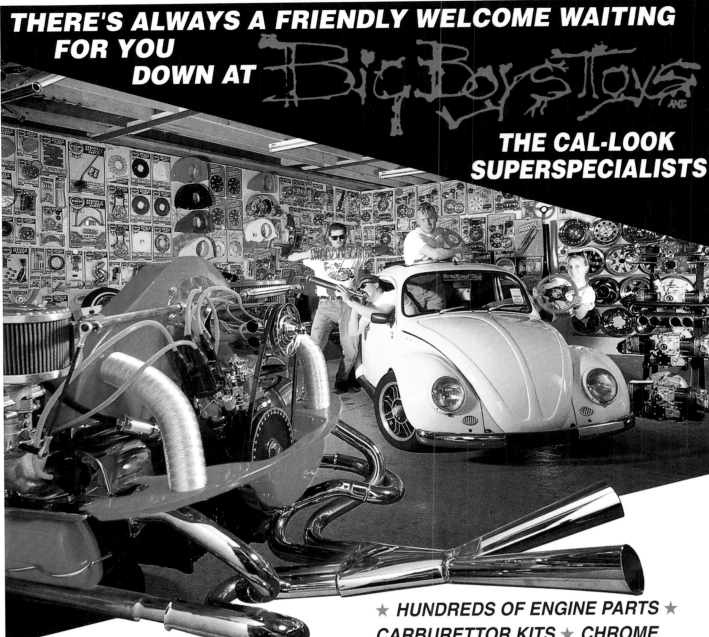

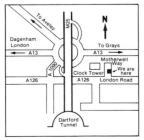

Choosing & Buying
your
VW BEETLE

293 JGW

Choosing & Buying your
VW BEETLE

Peter Noad

Windrow & Greene AUTOMOTIVE

Peter Noad driving his Car & Car Conversions-*sponsored Beetle on the 1971 Trident Rally, navigated by Sue Granger*

Published in Great Britain by
Windrow & Greene Ltd
19A Floral Street
London WC2E 9DS

A C.I.P. catalogue record for this book
is available from the British Library.

ISBN 1 85915 020 9

Designed by
ghk DESIGN,
10 Barley Mow Passage,
London W4 4PH

Advertising
Boland Advertising
Salatin House, 19 Cedar Road,
Sutton, Surrey SM2 5JG

Printed in Malta for
Amon-Re Ltd

The Author

When Peter Noad bought his first car he chose a VW Beetle because he saw one winning a rally in which it was able to climb a slippery snow-covered hill where most of the other cars had failed. He was misled into believing the car he bought was a 1956 Beetle, when in fact it was made much earlier — probably in 1946. This is a mistake he could have avoided if a book such as this had been available at the time!

Peter drove that split-window, cable-braked Beetle, and subsequently three newer examples, with great success in motorsport, winning a number of regional and national rally and autotest championships.

His first work as a journalist was to report on rallies and trials (in which he was also competing as a driver) for *Motoring News* and *Autosport*. He has been a regular contributor to *VW Motoring* magazine (formerly *Safer Motoring*) since 1966 and to *Volkswagen Audi Car* since 1982, as well as writing about VWs for other publications. He is the author of *VW Beetle in Motorsport*, published by Windrow & Greene.

He currently owns the Mexican-built Jubilee Beetle pictured on the front cover of this book, plus three Audi 80s. Aside from Volkswagens and Audis, his interests include jazz and cats.

Contents

INFORMATION PANELS

Author's Acknowledgements

I would like to thank Gene Berg, Christine Biggs, James Calvert (Stateside Tuning), Howard Cheese (Mexican-Brazilian Beetle Register), Peter Hedges, Hugh and Tricia Slater (Semi-Auto Beetle Register), Rod Sleigh (Historic VW Club), Peter Stevens and Suzy King (Autobarn), Geoff Thomas (Autocavan), Francis Tuthill and Roy Wilson, for help and information; all the owners of the cars pictured in the book, including George Allison, Robin Arkle, Roger Beasley, Eddie Butler, Colin Cockayne, Alf Faccenda, Jim McLachlan, Tony Middleditch, Jim Murray, Keith Seume, Bob Shaill, Derek Smith, Onno Termeulen and Iain Thompson; and the Volkswagen Press Department for the loan of test cars.

My thanks also go to Northway Garage Ltd in Wembley for their excellent service and for supplying parts for all my Volkswagens and Audis over the years; to the late Bob Wyse who, as editor of *Safer Motoring*, gave me my first opportunity to write extensively about my favourite cars; to Neil Birkitt, Robin Dow, John Forbes and Ken Green for sharing with me their enthusiasm for Beetles; to my brave companions Mick Hayward, Sue Granger, Mike Templeman, Alan Harmer, Tony Pryce, Dennis Crome and Brian Culcheth who accompanied me on rallies in my Beetles, TLC 116, 336 BGP, TKE 367H and SKT 328H; and to John Pendlebury for selling me his Jubilee Beetle, C107 NBV. I would also like to say a special thank you to Cindy Dodwell, Sandra Maskell and Stephanie Maskell.

Peter Noad

Except where otherwise credited, all photographs are by the author. The historic VWs pictured are privately-owned, restored cars, photographed within the last 20 years. Although they are believed to have been restored as faithfully as possible, strict authenticity in every detail cannot be guaranteed.

Background and assessment

Despite the fact that VW's biggest-selling car for almost two decades has been the Golf, there are still countless people to whom the name Volkswagen means Beetle and nothing else. Beetle production ceased in Europe in 1978, but enthusiasm and demand for it have not diminished. Beetles are still produced in Mexico at the rate of about 450 per day, there is a waiting-list of several months, and many Europeans have made the 10,000-mile round trip to Mexico to obtain a new Beetle by personal import! In 1993, production recommenced in Brazil.

Demand for Beetles is such that there is a growing industry engaged in restoring and 'remanufacturing' old Beetles and assembling 'new' cars from parts. A 25-year-old Beetle in good condition will demand a higher price than a five-year-old Ford Granada.

Undoubtedly the automobile phenomenon of the century, Volkswagen's Beetle has defied all its critics and sold to more people, in more countries, than any other car. During the 1960s and 1970s, Beetle production was more than a million a year (over 5,000 per day!) and it passed the long-standing record of the Ford Model T (15,007,033) in February 1972. At that time, Beetles were being sold in 150 different countries. By June 1992, the Beetle had raised the world record for production of a single model to 21 million.

The story of the Beetle began more than 60 years ago. It was in 1931 that Ferdinand Porsche made his first sketches of a 'people's car'. He believed a fundamentally new approach was needed: instead of the existing practice of scaling down bigger cars with their heavy steel or timbered frames, heavy water-cooled engines and leaf-sprung axles, Porsche's ideal small car was Beetle-shaped, with an air-cooled engine at the rear. The body was bolted to a steel floorpan with a central tunnel for stiffness, and it had all-independent suspension using the torsion bar system which Porsche had recently invented.

First Zündapp and then NSU expressed interest in Porsche's design, already known as a 'Volksauto', but for various reasons both abandoned the project. The German government then made it clear to the automobile industry that the motor car should not be reserved only for the privileged minority, but should be available to the working classes. As a result of this policy, Porsche's plans for his Volksauto received government backing in 1934 and the first prototype was completed at the end of 1935. Various engine configurations were tried, including two-cylinder and two-stroke designs, before settling on the now-famous flat four.

Three cars each completed 50,000 km of endurance tests in 1936, and the following year a further batch of 30 covered a combined total of 2.4 million km of testing. These pre-production cars had no back window at all (restricted vision was possible through the engine cooling slots), no

Above and left: The first 'production' versions of the Beetle were military vehicles. During the Second World War about 70,000 Volkswagens were produced, mostly Kubelwagens such as this example from 1945. These vehicles used Beetle engines and chassis. There were also four-wheel drive and amphibious versions. Some have survived and are now prized collector's items.

Left: A few hundred Beetle saloons were produced for military use from 1940 to 1945, mostly painted a matt sand colour. Some were adapted to run on wood and charcoal fuel.

When Did The Beetle Get Its Name?

In the beginning there was only one model. The Beetle was known simply as the Volkswagen or the VW. When the Convertible and Commercial models were added to the range in the early 1950s, the Beetle became the Volkswagen Sedan. In workshop manuals and factory documentation, it was described as Type 1.

The first use of the name Beetle may have been in England in 1950. There is a story that the nickname was given to John Colborne-Baber's VW (one of the first to be seen in England) by his son's school-friends.

Beetle was certainly not in general use as a name for the VW at that time. In fact, a team of Morris Minors was named 'The Beetles' on the Circuit of Ireland Rally in 1953. The word 'Beetle' certainly never appeared in magazine road tests in the early 1950s. In 1958, however, *Autosport* magazine referred to 'the victorious "beetles" on the Mobilgas Round Australia Rally'. From around that time, the name was occasionally used in print, but with a small 'b' and usually in inverted commas. Bill Boddy, the editor of *Motor Sport*, who did a great deal to publicise the Volkswagen during that period, sometimes referred to the car as a beetle.

It was probably the introduction of the Type 3, in 1961, which led to more general usage of the name Beetle for the Type 1. Official nomenclature identified Type 3 as VW 1500 and Type 1 as VW 1200, but as the model range increased with 1300 and 1500 engines in Type 1 a name became necessary to avoid confusion.

The VW was well-known as the Beetle when John Lennon and friends formed their famous pop group, after which it was sometimes mis-spelled as 'Beatle'.

In 1967, official *Volkswagenwerk* publications began to recognise the term 'Beetle', but it was still shown in inverted commas and the formal nomenclature remained VW 1200, VW 1300 etc. By 1969, the name Beetle had become the official generic term and appeared prominently in brochures and other publications.

The Americans, of course, have a different language (hood for bonnet, deck lid for engine cover etc), so they called the Beetle the 'Bug'. Nowadays both Beetle *and* Bug are used in the USA. In Germany the VW became *Der Käfer*, in France *La Coccinelle* (Ladybird), in Italy *Maggiolino* (Maybug), and in Norway *Bobla*.

running-boards or bumpers, and rear-hinged forward-opening doors. Plans for construction of the factory were completed in the same year.

The Beetle was ready to go into production in 1938. By then it had the split rear window and front-hinged doors, and looked identical to the early post-war examples that still exist today.

At the outbreak of war the factory was not quite completed, but in 1940 it began producing military reconnaissance vehicles (*Kübelwagen*), using the Beetle chassis and engine. By 1945, despite suffering severe bomb damage during the war, the factory had produced about 70,000 vehicles. Mostly these were *Kübelwagen* and the amphibious version, known as *Schwimmwagen*. Only 630 Beetle cars were made before 1945.

The immediate post-war resurrection of the Volkswagen factory in Wolfsburg has been well documented by automotive historians. British military officers — Major Ivan Hirst and Wing-Commander Dick Berryman — played a significant part in the rebirth of Beetle production, but the British motor industry dismissed the Volkswagen as totally unattractive to the average

motor-car buyer: it was said to be too ugly, too noisy, and to represent no competition to British cars in the world market!

By October 1946, 10,000 Beetles had been produced. In 1948 Heinz Nordhoff became Managing Director, and by 1951 VW had produced a quarter of a million vehicles and was exporting to 29 countries. The one million mark was reached in 1955, and the ten millionth Beetle was produced in 1967.

In its early years, the Beetle was vastly superior to contemporary small saloons such as the Morris Minor and Ford Anglia. It was not only technically unique, but was also unique in its reliability and ruggedness and its ability to negotiate rough roads and to be driven continuously at maximum speed. Although it was hardly a design criterion in the 1930s, the Beetle's resistance to rust is superior to 'modern' saloons due to its shape, and repair is easier due to the separate body and chassis construction.

Although one or two other manufacturers (for example, Fiat and NSU) copied the air-cooled rear-engine configuration, none truly copied the

Beetle. However, great advances were made by the automobile industry and by the mid-1970s water-cooled front-wheel-drive cars began to outclass the Beetle in terms of performance, road-holding, fuel consumption, heating and ventilation, interior space, noise level and servicing requirements. It took considerably longer, and the introduction of galvanising, to match the Beetle's long-term resistance to rust, and it took four-wheel drive to match the Beetle's ability to climb muddy or icy hills. In the 1990s, if you want a 'people's car' that will provide reliable, economical everyday transport and cover high mileages with the minimum of servicing, then the logical choice is a Golf Diesel, not a Beetle.

But Beetles now have many other roles and appeal to an extraordinarily diverse range of folk — from college kids with their mega-bass sound systems and funky graphics to wrinklies in wellies attempting to drive up muddy hills that have been unsuitable for motor vehicles since 1929; from historical experts who collect such items as semaphore indicators and dashboard-mounted bud vases to drag-racers with nitrous oxide injection and wheelie bars.

A substantial part of the VW scene is involved in customising. The Beetle is probably the world's most widely and best customised car. The now world-famous 'Cal-look' originated in southern California around 1968. After 25 years, it is still the most super-cool, hip, wicked, in-style shape on wheels. Many of those now building and buying Cal-look Beetles were not yet born when Cal-look began — and when VW had already sold ten million Beetles! It seems the Beetle, like jeans and rock'n'roll, will never go out of style.

It is thanks largely to the enthusiasm and loyalty of all those folk who are into customising that the VW parts, accessories, restoration and performance industry has the strength and depth which enable Beetles of any age to be maintained — whether for street, show or motorsport use — more easily and cheaply than any other classic car.

Beetles compete in almost all types of motorsport. They are modified to develop more than 400bhp for drag racing and rallycross. There are Beetles with turbos, four-wheel drive and 16 valves. All-Beetle circuit racing started in 1989 (with the Käfer Cup in Germany) and is so successful that it is spreading all over the world. The British version, the Big Boys' Toys Beetle Cup, was voted the second most popular of all types of motor racing by spectators at Brands Hatch in 1992. Beetles have for many years been the most widely used and successful production saloons in classic trials, where their ability to climb steep, muddy, rocky hills is surpassed only by purpose-built specials. In the 1950s and 1960s, Beetles regularly won outright the world's longest, roughest rallies, the East African Safari and the 10,000-mile Round Australia events.

Worldwide, there are probably more clubs, more get-togethers and more specialist magazines for Beetle enthusiasts than for any other single marque. In Britain alone, there are more than 100 clubs for air-cooled VWs.

Beetles have been involved in many amazing feats, such as removing and replacing the engine in less than two minutes and demonstrating the Beetle's ability to float by driving across various stretches of sea. In 1963, a Beetle was employed in Antarctica by a research expedition and out-performed both snow-track vehicles and dog-sledge teams.

Some Beetles have been bought as investments, as collectors' items to appreciate in value. This is especially true of the special limited editions and the last Convertibles in the late 1970s and early 1980s, little-used examples of which have now doubled or even trebled in value.

The most obvious bodywork differences that date a Beetle are the windows and headlamps. Up to March 1953, the Beetle had two small rear windows, popularly known as a 'split' window. (The reason for the dividing strip was that curved glass was not available.) From 1953 until August 1957, there was a one-piece, but still small, oval window. The larger, more rectangular rear window was introduced for the 1958 model year. In 1964, all the windows were slightly enlarged; this is most noticeable as narrower frames around the side windows. The trailing edge of the quarter vent window was also angled instead of being vertical.

A curved, so-called panoramic, windscreen was a feature of the 1303 model, introduced in 1972.

Vertical headlamps replaced the original sloping lamps in 1967. Other distinguishing features include the shape and size of tail lamps, type of turn signals and number of engine cooling vents; these are detailed in Chapter 3.

Significant mechanical changes occurred during the mid-1960s: ball joints replaced link-pins and king-pins in the torsion bar front suspension, and disc brakes and 12-volt electrics were introduced. The 1200cc engine remained in production, but 1300, 1500 and 1600cc versions evolved.

Beetles were traditionally known as VW 1200,

VW 1300 and VW 1500, according to engine size. Confusion was caused when Volkswagen changed the front suspension from torsion bars to MacPherson struts, fitted a 1600cc engine, and called it 1302S. It could not be called the VW 1600 because that designation already applied to the Type 3. The explanation of 1302S is that '02' signified a major chassis change to the 1300 and 'S' indicated a bigger engine. There was also a 1302 (not marketed in the UK) which consisted of the MacPherson strut chassis and 1300 engine, and there was a 1300S (also known as GT Beetle) with the torsion bar chassis and 1600 engine. There was never a 1301.

Initially the 1302S was called the Super Beetle in the UK. It was always known by that name in the USA.

When the final major change was introduced — a curved windscreen and completely redesigned facia — it became the 1303 (with 1300cc engine) and 1303S (with 1600cc engine).

Apart from the torsion bar or MacPherson strut front suspension, there are two different types of rear suspension. All use torsion bars, but the 1302, 1302S, 1303 and 1303S have double-jointed drive shafts with trailing wishbones, while the 1200, 1300 and 1500 have a simple swing-axle — except in the case of those with automatic transmission and post-1967 USA-spec models which have the double-jointed rear and torsion bar front.

The 1500 ceased production when the 1302S was introduced, but the 1200 and 1300 continued. The MacPherson strut '03' chassis went out of production with the last Convertible in 1980, but the torsion bar swing-axle '1200' chassis has endured and is still very much alive in the 1990s in Mexico. The latest development of the Mexican Beetle is the '1200' torsion bar, drum-braked chassis fitted with a 1600cc fuel-injection catalyst engine.

The Beetle has always been designated Type 1. Other related air-cooled VWs are Type 2, which is the Commercial/Delivery Van/Microbus/Motor Caravan, and Type 3 which is the Fastback, Notchback or Estate (called 'Variant' in Germany). Type 4 (the VW 411 or 412) is air-cooled but other than that has little in common with the Beetle. The Karmann Ghia (Type 14) and Convertible (Type 15) are directly based on the Beetle and have many common parts. Several other variations with different bodies were produced in Brazil.

Above: *The 1131cc 25bhp engine was produced from 1943 until the end of 1953.*

Which model to choose?

Split-window and oval-window Beetles and early Convertibles are nearly all in the hands of collectors (many in the USA and Japan) and are only offered for sale at collectors' prices. Most are rarely driven and only go on the road for occasional showing at *concours d'elegance*. A few are still being unearthed from time to time from barns, fields and junkyards around the world, in varying stages of decomposition, and are eagerly snapped up by enthusiasts with sufficient time and money to restore them. Some are sold in partially-restored condition when time, money or enthusiasm runs out.

Although the early models are highly regarded as collectable classics, the best purchase for everyday driving is a post-1968 model with practical features such as 12-volt electrics, disc

brakes, hazard warning flashers, mountings for rear seat belts, safety steering column and door locks and dual circuit brakes. By the late 1960s, the Beetle was very advanced in safety features, complying with American standards long before they became the norm for other European cars.

If left-hand drive is acceptable, you can have a very much newer Mexican-built Beetle. Until early 1986, Mexican Beetles were sold in Europe; these are especially worth buying as the later ones had a standard of rust-proofing commensurate with Volkswagen's six-year body warranty (as applicable to Golfs) and 'modern' components such as a heated rear window, laminated windscreen and inertia reel seat belts. It is possible to purchase a brand new Beetle by personal import from Mexico, but some modifications are necessary to 'Europeanise' it.

Motorsport Highlights

In the 1950s Beetles were the most successful cars in rallies and trials in Africa, Australia and Ireland. Beetles scored outright victories on the African Safari Rally in 1953, 1954, 1957 and 1962, the winning drivers being Alan Dix, Vic Preston Gus Hofmann and Tommy Fjastad, and on the Round Australia Rally (sponsored in turn by Redex, Ampol and Mobilgas) in 1955, 1956, 1957 and 1958, driven by Laurie Whitehead, Eddie Perkins, Jack Witter and Perkins (again).

These events, over distances up to 10,000 miles through mud, desert, jungle and boulder-strewn riverbeds, vied with each other for the title of 'the world's roughest, toughest and longest reliability trial'. Such was Volkswagen's syperiority that in 1957 Beetles took all top six places on the Mobilgas Round Australia Rally.

Paddy Hopkirk (later to achieve widespread fame with the Mini Coopers) and Kevin Sherry both became Irish trials/autotest champions driving Beetles, and Sherry was the outright winner of the Circuit of Ireland Rally in a Beetle in 1959, when he caused a sensation by beating the works Triumphs sports cars.

In later decades, Bill Bengry won the British National Rally Championship; Laurie Manifold and Peter Harrold became British Autocross Champions; Peter Noad won British Rally and Autotest Championships; Barry Ferguson won rally championships in Australia; Ken Shields dominated the Northern Ireland Autotest Championships; Mike Hinde, Ken Hoare, Mike Stephens and Dennis Greenslade won trials championships in Britain; Graham Hoare held the title of British Trials and Rally Drivers' Association All-Rounders Champion for nine years; Franz Wurz and Cees Teurlings won the European Rallycross Championship; Francois Monten held the Belgian Rallycross National title for many years; and Barry Ferguson, Peter Mill and Chris Heyer filled the top places in the Australian Rallycross Championship — all driving Beetles.

In the USA, Gene Berg, Dean Lowry and Joe Vittone were the first to put the VW on to the drag race strips, in the early 1960s. In 1987, Dave Perkins became the first to achieve 150mph on the quarter-mile drag strip in a Beetle. In 1994, Chris Bubetz became the new record-holder, achieving 152.8mph and an elapsed time of 8.3 seconds. In desert racing in the USA and Mexico, champions include the brothers Wayne, Darryl and Alan Cook, with their 1600cc Baja Beetle, and Martin Garribay with a Beetle in the production saloon class.

There are countless other drivers who have each collected hundreds of awards in various fields of motorsport. The fully illustrated history of VWs in competition is to be found in the present author's *VW Beetle In Motorsport*, published in 1992.

1200, 1300, 1500 or 1600?

Engine size is not really a major factor when choosing a used Beetle. All the engines are interchangeable and can be enlarged by fitting larger cylinder barrels and pistons and\or a longer stroke crankshaft. If the engine has done more than 70,000 miles, an overhaul is recommended and the opportunity can be taken to enlarge it if more power is required. The 1200 has a shorter stroke, but the 1300, 1500 and 1600 all have the same crankshaft with different cylinders and pistons.

1200, 1500 and pre-1971 1300 have single port heads; the 1600 and later 1300 have twin port heads. The twin port engines offer more scope for tuning, but in standard form have a carburettor and ignition system designed to reduce exhaust emissions, which can cause poor fuel consumption and flat spots in acceleration. Twin port heads seem to be more susceptible to cracking and, as capacity and power are increased, cooling becomes more critical.

Although performance of the 1200 Beetle is somewhat limited and one should not be over-ambitious when overtaking, especially approaching an uphill gradient, good examples will do considerably more than VW's quoted 'maximum and cruising speed' of 72mph, and the 1200 is the most economical Beetle.

The 1300 engine in the heavier 1302 or 1303 body is also rather limited in performance, and is not very economical.

Best performance is obtained from either the 1500 Beetle or the 1300S GT Beetle.

Above: *Trainloads of Beetles leaving the factory.*
(Volkswagen Press Department)

Right: *Enthusiasts have been modifying and customising Beetles since the 1960s. Custom Beetle shows remain as popular as ever; this is a scene from the VW Action festival in 1993.*

Previous page
Top: *Aerial view of the Volkswagen factory at Wolfsburg, taken in the 1960s.*
(Volkswagen Press Department)

Bottom: *Beetle production lines at Wolfsburg in the late 1960s. At its peak, the total worldwide production of Beetles was more than one million per year.*
(Volkswagen Press Department)

Left: In the days when its main rivals were Morris Minors and Ford Anglias, the Beetle enjoyed great success in motorsport. Peter Noad used this split-window, cable-braked Beetle as his first rally car, when it was already 15 years old. Pictured here are competitors waiting to start a section of the Hagley Car Club's Welsh 12-Hour Rally in 1961.

Below: Peter Noad's second Beetle, a 34bhp 1960 model, competing in a trial organised by the London Motor Club at Bordon in 1963. *(W & H Busby)*

Opposite page:
Top: One of the most successful Beetle drivers in motorsport was autocross champion Laurie Manifold, in action here in the Player's No 6 National Championship in 1968.

Insert: European rallycross saw the ultimate in motorsport Beetles. Pictured here at Brands Hatch in the 1985 Rallycross Grand Prix, Mikael Nordstrom's Beetle had a turbocharger, intercooler, twin overhead cam and four-wheel drive.

Bottom: Beetle engines and suspension compontents are widely used in buggies and 'rails' for off-road racing. They need to be tough to withstand this kind of activity!

Swing-axle or double-jointed rear?

Again, for most people this is not a deciding factor. Double-jointed rear suspension ultimately gives better handling than the swing-axle because there is less change of wheel camber angle. However, the Beetle's over-riding characteristic (like that of a Porsche) will always be dictated by the rear engine, which is responsible for an over-steering tendency and sensitivity to cross-winds.

Handling of the swing-axle Beetle was significantly improved when VW introduced the wider rear track and Z-bar in the mid-1960s. It is especially important with the swing-axle cars to have good quality shock absorbers and good tyres. Given these, the handling has proved quite good enough for rallying and the race-track. The Big Boys' Toys Beetle Cup race cars are all swing-axle models.

MacPherson strut or torsion bar front suspension?

By Beetle standards, the strut suspension models had a very brief production run. The 1302 was in production for only two years and the 1303 lasted only three years as a Beetle Sedan, although it did continue, in much smaller numbers, as a Convertible for a further five years. In time, the 1302 and 1303 will become the rarities of the Beetle family and one can expect parts which are unique to these strut suspension models to become less easily obtainable than parts for the torsion bar models. There are no problems in obtaining parts for the basic torsion bar swing-axle Beetle (1200, 1300 or 1500) which has been in production with few major changes for more than 30 years.

Below: Against-the-clock engine change contests are a feature of many VW club festivals. The Beetle engine can be removed and refitted in under two minutes!

Right: For many years Beetles were identified by their engine size and known as VW1200, VW1300 and VW1500. Confusion was caused when the first 1600cc Beetle was badged VW1302S.

Below: Early in the Beetle's history there was a commercial derivative, produced in delivery van, mini-bus, pick-up and other versions, which was known as Type 2 and used basically the same engine and transmission as the Beetle. This is a 1968 model second generation Transporter. Early models had a divided windscreen and hinged as opposed to sliding doors.

(Volkswagen Press Department)

Link–pin or ball-joint front suspension?

The ball-joint front suspension introduced in August 1965 is preferable because parts for the earlier link-pin/king-pin suspension are difficult to obtain. (Link-pin suspension is favoured for off-road racing because longer suspension travel is possible, but special parts are used.) It is not feasible to convert a link-pin car to ball-joint unless the car is the subject of a complete body-off restoration and the frame head can be replaced.

Six or 12 volts?

Dim lights, dodgy starting and non-availability of electrical accessories are just three disadvantages of six-volt Beetles. Conversion to 12 volts *can* be achieved, but it involves more than just replacing the battery, bulbs, turn signal flasher, wiper motor, dynamo, coil and starter: the 12-volt starter needs the larger flywheel, which in turn necessitates more clearance in the bell housing. (The six-volt starter can actually be used with a 12-volt system.)

Below: The Type 3 was Volkswagen's first attempt at a larger car. Still using the same design of air-cooled engine and torsion bar suspension, the Type 3 was produced in Notchback, Fastback and Estate Car (a.k.a. Variant) versions. Pictured is a 1968 1600L Variant.
(Volkswagen Press Department)

Disc or drum brakes?

When correctly adjusted and in good condition, the drum brakes work quite well. However, they require more pressure and more travel at the pedal than discs, and are more susceptible to the effects of water (after driving through floods) and overheating (when driving down long, steep hills). Conversion from drums to discs (only with ball-joint suspension) is quite easy and not too expensive.

Left-hand or right-hand drive?

Lhd to rhd is a conversion that should not be contemplated unless you are prepared to spend a great deal of money or already have comprehensive engineering facilities and expertise. There are many structural and safety considerations and the work will be scrutinised by your insurers. Conversion of earlier models posed fewer problems, but with the cessation of all rhd production in 1978, most of the 'ambidextrous' design features have been eliminated.

Many Beetle drivers in the UK, the author included, are perfectly happy with left-hand drive. It does attract an additional insurance premium (generally 25 percent), but a great many years would have to pass before this higher charge would equal the cost of a properly engineered conversion.

Right: The Karmann-Ghia, a sporty-looking coupé with standard Beetle engine and suspension, was manufactured at the Karmann factory in Osnabruck from 1955 to 1974. This is a 1967 1500.

Below: The Beetle's chassis is ideal as the basis for buggies and kit cars. The latter include some exotic-looking coupés such as this Charger.

Above: The best Beetle to purchase for everyday driving is a post-1968 model with 12-volt electrics and up-to-date safety features. The Beetle reached the peak of its development in the late 1960s and the cars produced in Mexico through the 1980s and into the 1990s are little changed from this 1969 model.

Left: It was only by joining forces with Audi NSU that Volkswagen was able to move out of the Beetle age. The Audi 80, launched in 1972, proved an outstanding success, both technically and commercially, and became the source of all Volkswagen's future water-cooled front-wheel drive developments.

2

Buying a Beetle — what to look for

Before looking at a Beetle with a view to purchase, you need to decide exactly why you are buying it. As everyday transport? As a 'classic' car which will be used only on special occasions and displayed at shows? Or as a car for competitive events such as trials, rallies and races? You will also need to think about how much time and money you are prepared to spend on the car after you have bought it.

You need to understand the jargon used in the advertisements. *Original* should mean that the car has Volkswagen factory components throughout, all of the correct model year. Unless it has been stored in a museum, most of the 'original' components are likely to be rusty or worn out.

Restored should mean that rusty and worn out components have been replaced by genuine Volkswagen parts applicable to the car's model year and that, both mechanically and cosmetically, its condition is virtually indistinguishable from when it first left the showroom umpteen years ago. In reality, 'restored' can cover all manner of bodge-ups and might mean little more than that the car has been repaired sufficiently to obtain an MOT certificate.

If you are considering a Beetle as a *classic car*, then originality or authentic restoration is of paramount importance. It must have all the right parts for its year — the correct bumpers, the correct shape of tail lamps, a standard engine of the correct type, and so on. The paintwork and

upholstery must be of a colour that was available at the time the car was manufactured, and only factory-approved accessories of the period may be fitted — a classic car of the 1960s does not have 100-watt stereo!

Concours implies that the car is good enough to satisfy the judges at a *concours d'elegance*. This will mean that the bodywork and interior (including luggage boot and engine compartment) are visually near-perfect and either original or superbly restored. If the car does truly meet this description, then it will command a very high price. A concours winner is worth £3,000-£4,000 more than an equivalent model which is merely in top condition according to a used car price guide. Do bear in mind, though, that concours competitions are static and there is no guarantee that a concours car's internal mechanical condition or dynamic qualities will match its appearance.

Customised is the converse of 'original' or 'classic'. It means that the car looks different from any other and has a large number of non-standard parts, which might range from fancy paintwork and a retrimmed interior to a lowered roof and highly modified engine. Customising is often all about visual effect and takes little or no account of functionality — the car might be totally impractical as a vehicle!

Most Beetles that are bought and sold do not fall into any of these categories. They are regarded as *daily drivers*, i.e. cars for everyday use, albeit within the limitations of the Beetle's basic design. There are likely to be non-original, non-genuine replacement parts, a greater or lesser degree of mechanical deterioration, and there will certainly be some rust.

The Beetle's resistance to rust was basically quite good; it was certainly better in that respect than other cars designed in the 1930s and 1940s, and probably better than most cars up to the 1970s or 1980s. The rounded shape enables water to run off and there are not too many nooks and crannies to harbour corrosive accumulations of mud. Thickness of the original metal has always been very generous and the factory-applied paint finish was second to none, at least until the mid-1970s when problems with metallic paint appeared. The separate body-chassis construction and bolt-on wings make for easier repair, and if rust does take hold it is seldom fatal.

Nevertheless, most Beetles are now very old and one must expect serious rust on any car manufactured ten, 20 or more years ago. During that length of time, the car is likely to have been involved in accidents and been repaired with poor quality materials, to have been left with accumulations of mud and salt adhering to it, enclosed in a garage when it was wet, or exposed to sunlight for long periods which causes rubber seals to perish. Any of these factors will have promoted corrosion.

The two most likely causes of rust are splits in the rubber seals around the windows which allow water to seep down inside the metal panels, and blocked drainage holes which prevent any water from escaping.

The most serious places for rust to occur are the floorpan, sills, frame head and door pillars. However, even in these key areas, severe corrosion is not necessarily cause for a Beetle to be written off. Replacement panels are available for every part of a Beetle body and chassis, and because of the relatively high (some might say inflated) value of Beetles, it is often viable to repair a rotten example which if it were of any other make would be worthless.

For instance, one can spend £4,000 restoring an old Beetle, purchased for £500, and it will be worth £5,000. The real risk lies in buying a Beetle for £4,000 that is supposedly rust-free and fully restored, only to discover subsequently that the work has been done badly and that it will take a further £4,000 to make it good.

It is better to buy a car with obvious rust, at a low price, than a supposedly restored more expensive example, with hidden rust. The secondhand Beetle market contains a great many of the latter!

In addition to the possibility of rust hidden beneath filler or dubious tacked-on patches, there is the likelihood of cheap 'pattern' repair panels being used which are thinner gauge metal, of inferior quality, with a poor standard of priming and painting. The Beetle's reputation and value spring from its durability, ruggedness and build quality, but there are many people out there who are 'repairing' Beetles with metal that barely has the quality or ruggedness of a baked beans can!

When inspecting a potential purchase, the first place to look for rust, or for signs of dubious repair, is underneath the back seat. This is where the battery is located, with its inherent possibility of acidic fumes or leakage, and it is the area where any water that has leaked into the car will remain. There have been many cases where the battery has almost literally fallen through a hole in the floor.

Look underneath the car to see if the pattern of ribbing is the same on both sides of the floor. If the ribbing is different, it is a sure sign that one side has been replaced with an aftermarket repair panel or, worse still, plated over. Lift the rubbery mats and inspect the entire area of the floor inside the car, looking for rust, dampness and tacked-on patches. At the same time, check the hydraulic brake line which runs alongside the tunnel on the driver's side. Although enclosed inside the car, this is prone to corrosion and ultimate fracture. The fuel line should be inside the tunnel; if a new fuel pipe is visible, having been routed outside the tunnel, this indicates a corrosion problem in the frame head at the tunnel's front end.

The sills are part of the body, as distinct from the chassis/floorpan. Chassis-to-body attachment is by bolts between the sills and the perimeter of the floorpan. The most obvious sign of corrosion in the sill is a jacking point that is weak or out of position, usually associated with a kink in the running board. A simple test is to ask the vendor to jack the car up, using the standard jack: if the jack distorts the running board, while the wheels stay on the ground, you can be sure that new sills are needed.

Air for heating the car flows through the sills, so another test is to see if there is a plentiful supply of air from the heater. If not, then there is either a hole or a blockage due to corrosion of the sills. It is important to check that hot air reaches the demisting slots at the windscreen, as well as the footwell outlets.

While driving with the heater on, you can check for any fumes. A 'hot metal' smell is normal. Any leaks of exhaust, oil or petrol will be detectable as fumes through the heater.

While inspecting the underside of the car, you should check that the drainage holes in the bottom of the sills are not blocked. (Note that there are also ventilation holes in the top of the sill, visible when the door is opened, the purpose of which is to enable air to flow through the sill, forced by the pressurising effect of closing the door.)

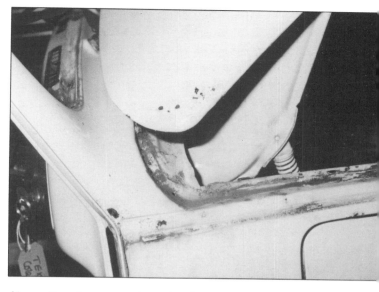

Above: *Rusty bonnets can be replaced relatively cheaply, but any sign of corrosion at the base of the windscreen or in the pillar or scuttle is serious.*

Left: *Rust at the edge of the quarter panel by the door pillar indicates that the pillar itself is also corroded and the car will need a complete body-off restoration.*

Below: *Serious rot at the base of the door pillar will invariably be accompanied by rotten sills. It is likely to be hidden by filler and paint but you should be suspicious of this area if the heating and demisting are poor. This example has a typical patch welded on to the sill which is normally hidden by the running board.*

Look also at the frame head, which is at the front end of the chassis beneath the petrol tank. There is a drain tube from the fresh air box which passes under the luggage compartment liner and goes down behind the tank. If this becomes damaged (due, for example, to heavy objects in the luggage boot), water can accumulate and rot the area beneath and behind the tank. Lift out the luggage boot liner and check the drain tube.

Also inspect the front torsion bar assembly. The end pieces, which join the two torsion bar tubes and provide the top mounting for the shock

Above: Rust tends to start at the wing attachment points. Rust at the bottom corner of the wheel arch is a continuation of the sill problem.

Left: Like the rear wing attachment points and bumper mountings, the corner of the bodywork immediately above the rear suspension torsion bar is a common rusting point.

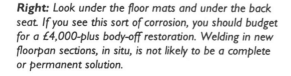

Right: Look under the floor mats and under the back seat. If you see this sort of corrosion, you should budget for a £4,000-plus body-off restoration. Welding in new floorpan sections, in situ, is not likely to be a complete or permanent solution.

absorber, are susceptible to rust if the drain holes are blocked. The complete torsion bar front suspension (known as the front axle beam) is simply bolted on, by four bolts to the frame head and two body-mounting bolts, and can be easily replaced.

On the 1302 and 1303 models with strut front suspension, the frame head is completely different and carries mountings for the track control arms and anti-roll bar, while the coil spring struts have their mountings in the bodywork, at each side of the luggage compartment. Corrosion of the bodywork in this area is therefore more serious than it would be on a torsion bar model.

In the main bodyshell, the most likely areas of rust are at the bottom of the panel between the door and rear wheel arch, just above the suspension arm, the lower rear corner inside the front wheel arch, around the bumper mountings and inside the spare wheel compartment. Rust at the bottom of the door pillar is likely if you have found extensive corrosion elsewhere, and obviously it is serious. It is usually associated with rotten sills and perished windscreen rubbers. Poor heater flow to the screen vents is a symptom of rusted sills at the base of the door pillars. Attempting to lift the door when open will reveal any weakness of the pillar and door hinges. You should, of course, check the bottom of the doors for rust, although Beetles are probably not as bad in this area as many other cars.

Look carefully for bodged repairs with filler or crude patching and plating. We have seen Beetles with literally dozens of little patches welded on, particularly inside the wheel arches, presumably (as previously noted) to cover up each hole as it appears in order to get through the next MOT test. Inevitably the surrounding areas will also be rusty and the entire panel will need replacing.

To deal with any serious rust it is necessary to remove the body from the chassis. Repairs attempted without removing the body can, at best, simply conceal the problem from a gullible would-be buyer. Any welding of the sills or adjacent areas will melt, or seriously damage, the seal between the body and the floorpan, allowing water and mud to get in and cause more corrosion. We've seen Beetles with plates welded across the join, tacked to both body and floorpan. This is extremely bad practice: it will not be rustproof for very long and it makes subsequent removal of the body, to do the job properly, that much more difficult.

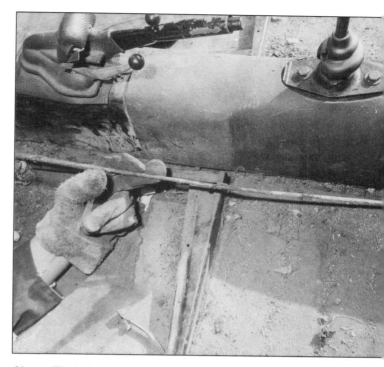

Above: The hydraulic line to the rear brakes is prone to corrosion where it runs beneath the front seat.

Above: A badly corroded and patched torsion bar front axle beam. Corrosion of the uprights is accelerated when the drainage holes become blocked. The complete beam can be replaced quite easily — an advantage of the torsion bar Beetle over the strut suspension model.

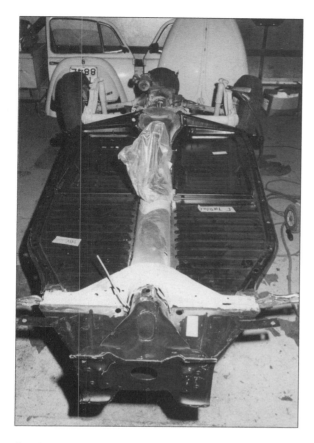

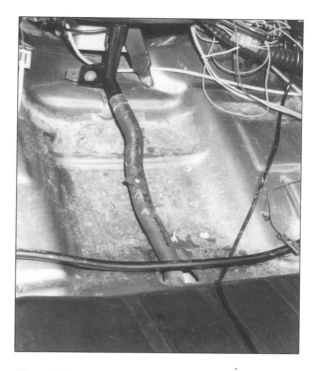

Above: This is the water drain tube from the fresh air ventilation intake in front of the windscreen. It passes beneath the luggage compartment liner and any damage sustained can result in water accumulating in the area behind and beneath the petrol tank, inevitably leading to corrosion.

Previous page and above: A proper restoration job should involve removal of the body from the chassis so that new floorpans and framehead can be fitted, as seen in this example of work in progress in Francis Tuthill's workshop. If a car is advertised as being fully restored, you should expect to see photographic evidence of this type.

Below: A view from beneath the engine showing the pushrod tubes and thermostat in the righthand-side cooling duct outlet. Oil leaks can occur from the pushrod tubes.

Above: Slight oil seepage from the rocker boxes is not uncommon and not serious. It can be rectified for a few pence by obtaining and fitting (correctly) a new cork gasket. This car is a stick-shift automatic with the ATF reservoir under the righthand-side rear wing, with a hose connection to the special oil pump. This should be free of leaks.

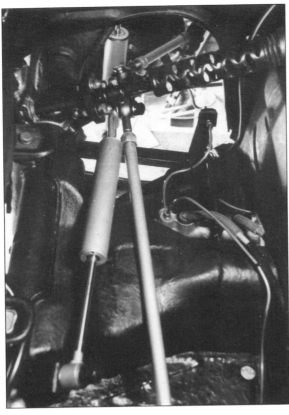

Above: A view beneath the petrol tank from the lefthand front wheel arch, showing the framehead, steering damper and brake master cylinder. This is Christine Biggs' Beetle, which has been rebuilt to concours standard. The area shown is susceptible to corrosion on a neglected car and should be inspected thoroughly, as an ineffective steering damper will cause severe steering oscillations. The damper can easily be replaced; an upgrade to a Koni (as fitted to this car) is recommended. (Christine Biggs)

Below: Be wary of lowered suspension and a non-standard exhaust. If taken to extremes in the interests of customising, the loss of ground clearance can render the car totally impractical.

The engine

Although Beetle enthusiasts regard the air-cooled 'never freezes, never boils, no leaking hoses' engine as being almost sacred, it has to be said that the engine is, in fact, one of the Beetle's main weaknesses. In order properly to explain what the prospective buyer should be looking for, it is necessary first to describe the engine's characteristics and some of its common defects.

VW Motoring magazine has a register of readers' cars that have covered more than 100,000 miles, and this includes a record of whether the engine is original or has been replaced. Analysis of this data reveals the rather telling statistic that, of the air-cooled VWs reaching 100,000 miles, 40 percent have needed a new engine. The corresponding figure for water-cooled models (Polo, Golf, Passat, Scirocco and Audi) is only two percent.

The problem with air-cooling is that, without a mass of water to act as a heat sink, the localised peak temperatures and transient fluctuations of temperature can be very much greater. And, with no water to boil and act as a warning indicator, overheating goes unnoticed until serious damage occurs — possibly resulting in seized pistons, dropped valves, cracked heads and distorted crankcase. Again, leakage of water, although a nuisance, is a visible warning; leakage of air will pass unnoticed until it is too late.

Ideally, the Beetle should have a temperature gauge for each cylinder head, but these instruments are not easily obtainable and fitment of the sensors can be tricky. The only other temperature indicator is an oil temperature gauge and this instrument is a highly recommended accessory.

The Beetle's oil temperature increases directly with the car's speed. When cruising on a motorway, the temperature is higher than when climbing hills at maximum power in low gears. The reason for this is that the air intake in the engine lid faces rearwards and, at high forward speed, this is a region of low pressure.

Although it has always been said that the Beetle's maximum speed is cruising speed, and it has a low-revving, supposedly lightly-stressed engine, the truth is that the Beetle, at 75mph and 4000rpm, is very much closer to its temperature limit and stress limit than a Golf or Audi would be at 120mph and 6000rpm.

While the water-cooled engines happily

Buyer's Check List

When you are looking at a secondhand car with a view to purchase, it is easy to get carried away by enthusiasm or distracted by the vendor and overlook what might be major defects. Only if you work systematically through a check list will you ensure that important items are not forgotten, and, at the same time, establish yourself as someone who will not be 'conned' into making an unwise purchase. The following are essential items to include on your check list:

1. Is the car the correct model as advertised? Are the documents in order: vehicle registration (log book), service history (if claimed), MOT certificate? Is the chassis number correct for the stated model year?
2. Does the car have 12-volt electrics, right-hand drive and disc brakes? If not, are you prepared to accept its limitations?
3. Is the car standard or modified? If it is modified, is it what you really want or will there be problems with ground clearance, accessibility, insurance, fuel consumption etc?
4. Does the bodywork appear sound and free from rust? Check for signs of filler and welded-on patches, especially at the base of quarter panels and inside wheel arches.
5. Is the floorpan free of rust? Check beneath the mats/carpets and under the rear seat. Are the mats and carpets dry?
6. Are the sills and door pillars solid and free of rust? Inspect the jacking points. Check that the doors fit and open and close properly.
7. If the car has been 'restored', did the work include removal of the body from the chassis? What new parts were fitted and are they genuine VW parts?
8. Are there any signs of accident/damage repair?
9. Are the window rubbers in good condition?
10. Are the hoses, seals and tinware in the engine compartment all in good order?
11. Is the vendor familiar with the servicing requirements? Has he been using the correct oil and changing it at the recommended intervals?
12. Is the engine free from suspicious noises, oil leaks and fumes?
13. Does the oil pressure warning light operate correctly?
14. Does the heater operate effectively?
15. Does the clutch work smoothly without slipping?
16. Do all the gears engage smoothly and quietly?
17. Does the car run straight ahead with the steering wheel in the straight ahead position?
18. Are the brakes effective without juddering and pulling to one side?
19. Is there sufficient tread on all tyres? Are they all of the same size and type?
20. Is the condition of the interior acceptable?
21. Do the electrics all work? Check the lights, wipers, indicators, horn.
22. Are there any non-standard electrical gadgets? If so, does the wiring appear satisfactory?

operate continuously at an oil temperature of 130 degrees C, or up to 150C if synthetic oil is used, it is not really safe to run the Beetle engine with oil temperature above 110C. This is due not so much to a lubrication problem as to a temperature limit for the crankcase material: if it gets too hot, it loses strength and distorts.

The Beetle engine was designed to run on straight monograde oil; not multigrades and not synthetics. The oil cooler circuit is controlled by a pressure valve, not a thermostat, so it depends on the oil viscosity (and thus pressure) falling as temperature rises. If multigrade or synthetic oil is used, with a high viscosity index, the engine will 'think' the oil is less hot than it is. The cooler will therefore come into operation later, and the engine will actually run hotter.

The Beetle does not have a proper oil filter — it merely utilises something resembling a tea-strainer. Consequently, the oil must be changed frequently — ideally, every 2,000 miles. (An oil filter has been introduced in Mexican-built Beetles, starting in 1993). Oil capacity is small — only 4½ pints — so the level must be checked frequently. When cornering, the oil which is pumped to the rocker boxes to lubricate the valve gear is prevented, by centrifugal force, from returning to the crankcase via the pushrod tubes. If the level of oil is low, insufficient will remain in the crankcase to supply the pump, resulting in oil starvation at the crankshaft bearings.

The design and correct fitment of the fan housing and ducting are crucial to the maintenance of adequate cooling. Any gaps in the

Above: A 'tin-opener job' convertible. The door frame has been chopped off at the top of the quarter vent and at the base of the B-pillar. The single-layer canvas top is supported by three hoops which will be seen inside the car, and secured by press studs or Dzus fasteners. The rear window is plastic. Compare this with the genuine Karmann convertibles in the photos immediately following.

Left: A 'flat screen' 1300, 1500 or 1302S Karmann Cabriolet looks like this. The doors differ from those on a Beetle saloon — note the deeper section between the waistline and the base of the window, squared-off quarter window and full chrome surrounds to all side windows. There are no press-studs and the outline of the top is far smoother.

Right: A 'curved screen' 1303S Karmann Cabriolet. Apart from the windscreen frame, the top is virtually identical to that on the previous Karmann Cabrio. The rear window is again glass, with electric demisting on later models.

sheet metal, or damaged or missing rubber seals, which allow cooling air to escape will cause over-heating, and this will be exacerbated if the leaked hot air is sucked back in by the fan and recirculated.

When hot, the engine should not be switched off immediately but should be allowed to idle for a couple of minutes, so that a continuing flow of cooling air can reduce and stabilise the temperatures.

Valves are a weakness, especially the number three (front left) exhaust valve which usually runs the hottest; a dropped valve is a common cause of engine failure in Beetles. Valve clearances should be checked regularly — again, preferably every 2,000 miles — and it is recommended to replace the valves after no more than 60,000 miles.

There are other problems with this 1930s-design engine: both fuel economy and performance are relatively poor, there is some doubt concerning the use of unleaded petrol, and exhaust emissions are not good.

Of course, the Beetle engine can be, and often is, modified. Performance can be improved, but even bringing it to the level of a Golf Diesel requires fairly radical modifications and it is unlikely that any improvements will be achieved in fuel consumption, emissions or durability.

The redeeming features of the engine are that it is easy to remove and replacements are inexpensive. Exchange 'short' engines (comprising crankcase, cylinders, pistons, heads, oil pump, valve gear — but excluding fan, dynamo, carburettor and exhaust) cost around £500 from suppliers such as Autocavan and Volkspares, or about £850 from the VW factory.

If you are buying a Beetle with more than 50,000 miles on its existing engine, then you would be well advised to budget for a replacement engine. You can form some judgment of the present engine's condition by asking such questions as 'How often is the oil changed?', 'How often are the valve clearances checked?' and 'What type of oil is used?' (It should be a straight monograde 30, such as Castrol CRI 30.)

The presence of an oil temperature gauge would boost confidence. But any gaps in the cooling ducting, a slack fanbelt, a damaged rubber seal around the perimeter of the engine compartment, missing rubbers from the sparking plug caps, or a missing preheat hose, would cast considerable doubts on the engine's life expectancy.

Above: *Damaged Cabriolet tops can be professionally repaired, but you are advised to get a quote for any repairs before deciding whether or not to purchase a car in need of them.*

Most Beetle engines show signs of oil underneath and minor leakage need not give rise to concern. Drips from the front of the crankcase indicate leakage past the crankshaft oil seal which will mean that, sooner or later, oil will get on to the clutch and cause it to slip or drag. Replacement of the clutch plate and oil seal is not a big job. The engine has to be removed, but that can be accomplished in a matter of minutes!

Oil leaking at the side of the crankcase is likely to come from the pushrod tubes. Replacement of the standard tubes necessitates removal of the cylinder head(s), but there are telescopic tubes which can be fitted with the heads and engine *in situ*.

Although it is normal for the engine to sound 'tappety', there should not be any heavy knocking or rumbling noises, nor any rattles which vary with load or revs. Remove each spark plug lead in turn, when the engine is idling, and the revs should drop by a similar amount. Little or no change in revs when one spark plug is inoperative indicates the cylinder is doing very little work, which means that compression is low, due probably to a burnt valve. (With twin carbs, it can simply mean that the carbs are not balanced.)

Check that the oil pressure warning light does not come on at idling when the engine is warm (having initially checked that the light works when the ignition is first switched on). Ideally, in order to get the engine up to full temperature, you need to drive for several miles at maximum speed —say 70mph. When driving in town, neither the engine nor the oil reaches full working temperature and faults such as low oil pressure might not be apparent.

A little exhaust smoke on start-up is not a cause for concern — horizontally opposed engines are liable to retain oil in the combustion chamber or rocker box when standing — but you should not see any smoke thereafter when blipping the throttle. Take a look at the dipstick: if the oil is very black, or the level is well below the top mark, this indicates that servicing has been neglected. And check the fanbelt tension: if it is too slack, this also indicates neglect.

Beware of modified Beetles. With a non-standard carburettor, or twin carbs, the normal preheat hose to the air cleaner is usually removed and the resulting hole in the sheet metal above the exhaust must be sealed to avoid overheating. Throttle linkages and the hookup to the accelerator cable often leave something to be desired as regards long-term reliability. Non-original fuel hose connections should also be inspected closely. Accessibility can be a problem with twin carbs: it is often difficult or even impossible to get at the front pair of spark plugs.

A popular tweak, supposedly to give more power to the wheels, is to reduce the speed of the fan by fitting a smaller pulley on the crankshaft. While this has some benefit in short-duration motorsport, such as drag racing, in normal road use it causes overheating and is detrimental to crankshaft balance if the pulley is lighter than the original.

Major modifications, including increased capacity using big bore cylinders or long stroke cranks, should be accompanied by an extra oil cooler, uprated oil pump and full instrumentation. Larger valves or a high lift camshaft should be accompanied by stronger pushrods and rockers. Remember that many modified Beetles are built purely for show purposes — at least one list of engine 'tuning' accessories starts with items such as a chrome-plated dipstick! — and they are rarely driven far or fast.

Non-standard exhausts and lowered suspension will seriously reduce clearance and ground on the slightest ramp. Wide wheels, with excessive positive offset, will cause the steering to pull to one side whenever one wheel encounters a bump, puddle, or uneven braking force.

Beetles are not prone to gearbox faults: the transmission is virtually bullet-proof. Reverse gear is sometimes noisy, but the forward gears should be quiet, with unbeatable syncromesh. At 20mph you should be able to declutch and flick the lever into any of the synchronised gears as fast as you can move your hand, without any mechanical protest. Accelerate hard and then take your foot off to check that there is no jumping out of gear on the overrun.

If there *is* a gearbox fault, you should allow sufficient funds for a professional repair. Rebuilding the Beetle gearbox requires special tools and precise measurements and is not a job for the average DIY person.

The inner universal joints of the swing-axle are actually inside the gearbox. If the rubber gaiter is damaged, it will allow oil to leak from the gearbox, but this is easy to rectify. A repair kit is available using a split gaiter, fastened with screws, which can be fitted *in situ*.

Look behind the rear brakes: signs of oil on the backplate (on a swing-axle model) indicate that the hub oil seal is leaking and should be replaced, to prevent gearbox oil getting on to the brake linings. This is not a serious or expensive pro-

Below: This is the full toolkit supplied with an early 1970s Beetle, including a spare fanbelt. The correct toolkit and driver's handbook are essential for the serious concours competitor.

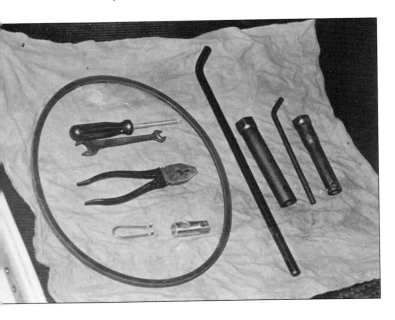

blem, but could be a useful bargaining point. So could worn shock absorbers, which on bumpy roads cause the suspension to bounce excessively.

Check that the steering does not pull to one side, both in steady driving and when braking, and that the steering wheel is in the straight-ahead position when the car is driven along a straight road. If possible, try starting on a hill and see if the clutch judders or slips. Judder can be caused by insufficient slack in the cable, but can also be indicative of oil on the clutch, problems with the pressure plate, or weak mountings of engine or transmission.

'New' Beetles

Several firms are now selling 'remanufactured' Beetles. These are cars that have been restored from wrecks with rust and/or accident damage. They look very nice — almost like brand-new — and are sometimes offered with mildly customised interiors and eye-catching paintwork. Prices generally start at around £5,000.

Standards vary, of course, so it is worth asking the vendor such questions as 'Did the restoration involve removal of the body?', 'Have genuine Volkswagen factory parts been used?' and 'To what extent have mechanical components, particularly steering, brakes and engine, been overhauled or renewed?'

It is possible to buy a complete brand-new Volkswagen factory-made chassis, and as this only costs about £600 it is not only better but also more cost-effective than welding in new floorpans. Also available are brand-new Volkswagen factory-made Beetle bodyshells, complete with doors, bonnet, engine lid and wings, for £2,644 (1200/1300 Beetle only; not 1302 or 1303). These, and many other genuine VW factory parts, are obtainable in the UK from Autobarn (see Chapter 6 for addresses of specialists).

Autobarn have, in fact, built complete Beetles from all brand-new parts, which cost about £16,000. Such a Beetle is vastly superior to any welded-up restoration costing half that amount and a further advantage is that it can be built to the customer's individual specification.

Another way of acquiring a new Beetle is to effect a personal import from Mexico. New Beetles only cost the equivalent of about £5,000 in that country, and by the time you have added the

Above: *Unless you are prepared to accept inferior handling, you should choose a Beetle with either double-jointed rear suspension or the swing-axle with Z-bar. The Z-bar can easily be recognised by the linkage seen here, which is attached to the axle rearwards of the shock absorber. It is important to have good shock absorbers on the swing-axle suspension; check for leaks and effective damping. Also check behind the brake drums for oil leaks which indicate a worn hub seal allowing oil to escape from the gearbox and along the axle tube.*

cost of travel, hotels, shipping, customs and charges and VAT, the total UK price becomes about £7,000 — still better value for money than most secondhand restored examples. The 1993 Mexican Beetle is a 1600cc torsion-bar model with fuel injection, electronic ignition and catalyst. Features include a laminated windscreen and fire extinguisher, but not (currently) a heated rear window or underseal.

Some modifications are necessary to comply with UK legislation, particularly with regard to the lights; and, of course, all the cars are left-hand drive. At the present time, there is a waiting-list of about six months.

A step-by-step guide on how to obtain a new Mexican Beetle has been produced by the Mexican/Brazilian Beetle register (see Chapter 6 for club addresses). Copies are available for £3,

plus a large SAE. The Register secretary receives about 100 inquiries each year, so there is quite a significant demand for new Mexican Beetles.

Some independent firms in Germany have started selling new Beetles imported from Mexico. Again, information can be obtained from the Mexican/Brazilian Beetle Register.

Beetle Convertibles

Prospective buyers of Beetle Convertibles must be aware of the difference between two types. *Real* Beetle Convertibles, or Cabriolets as they are known, were built by Karmann. The construction and quality of the soft top have been likened to those of a Rolls-Royce convertible: it has a multi-layer top, fully insulated, with a headlining which makes the interior look just like that of a saloon with no visible struts or folding mechanism. With the soft top closed, the car is just as weatherproof and quiet as a saloon, and still has a real glass rear window which, on later models, includes electric demisting. The rear side windows, also glass with chrome frames, wind down fully.

When open, the folded top is necessarily quite bulky. Its appearance helps to give the Beetle Cabrio its unique character, but, for short drivers

Above: A left-hand-drive Beetle, or one which has been converted from lhd to rhd, should not be bought without due consideration. Conversion is neither easy nor cheap, and poorly-converted cars should definitely be avoided. If you can cope with driving 'from the wrong side', there's nothing wrong with buying a lhd Beetle and keeping it unaltered. Insurance will be a little higher, but not by so much as to offset the cost of conversion, while the purchase price of the car should be lower and some parts and accessories might be easier to obtain for lhd than rhd.

in particular, rearwards visibility is somewhat obstructed.

Another important feature of the Karmann Beetle Cabriolet is that the body and sills are strengthened to compensate for the loss of rigidity due to the open top. This can be seen by looking at the bottom of the door opening: on the Beetle saloon this has square corners, while on the Cabriolet the corners between sill and door pillar are rounded, with strengthening fillets. The sills beneath the running-board are also visibly deeper and there is an extra cross-beam under the rear seat. This strengthening goes a long way towards eliminating the scuttle shake and rattles that afflict most open-top cars when driving on rough roads.

The Cabriolet often had a more advanced and luxurious specification than a Beetle saloon of the same year. American-spec. left-hand-drive Cabrios are quite common in Britain — certainly more so than American-spec. Beetle saloons. The high value of Cabrios more than compensates for importation costs, and those from California, where the climate is benign, are usually commendably free from rust. Late models have fuel-injection engines.

The Cabriolet top is susceptible to deterioration and attack by vandals, but there are specialists who can repair and re-skin the soft top. Addresses of these, and of fuel injection specialists, can be obtained by joining the Volkswagen Cabriolet Owners' Club, whose address can be found in Chapter 6.

The other type of Beetle convertible is the 'tin-opener' job, where someone has simply cut off the roof of a saloon and substituted a folding canvas top. At best, this is like the MG Midget — a draughty ragtop with rods and links showing inside and a plastic rear window which soon becomes scratched and discoloured. At worst, it offers little more protection from the elements than an umbrella.

Reputable converters have attempted to strengthen the lower part of the body, but the results are always cruder and less effective than the Karmann-built cars.

Genuine Karmann Beetle Cabriolets are very highly valued and command prices which may be £2,000 or £3,000 more than an equivalent Beetle saloon. Conversely, a 'tin-opener' convertible is almost always worth less.

Automatic Beetles

The automatic transmission fitted to Beetles is only semi-automatic and is sometimes known as 'auto stick-shift' or 'selector automatic'. In principle it is similar to the Sportomatic transmission on the Porsche 911. There is a conventional-looking gear lever but no clutch pedal. The gear lever operates only three forward speeds and the automatic electro-pneumatic clutch is triggered by moving the gear lever. There is a torque converter and it is possible to start off and drive all the time using only third gear. Better acceleration is achieved by shifting through all three gears.

Semi-automatic was first available on 1968-model 1500 and 1300 Beetles and continued through to end of production of the 1303S Cabriolet. The only version sold in any numbers in the UK was the 1500, and even these are quite rare now. Although acceleration is a little slower than with manual transmission, semi-auto Beetles are pleasant to drive: the gearchange is extremely quick, and in the case of the 1500/1300 roadholding is better because the automatic has double-jointed rear suspension instead of the manual car's swing-axle.

By all accounts, the automatic transmission is both reliable and durable. The clutch tends to be longer-lasting than on a manual car because it is automatic and not subjected to misuse by the driver.

If the clutch does not operate and the gears crunch, the most likely cause is the switch in the base of the gear lever. Cleaning the contacts will

Right: Lift out the luggage compartment liner and inspect the wiring behind the dashboard, especially if the car has been converted from lhd to rhd or if electrical accessories have been installed. This Mexican Beetle was converted to rhd by Peter Hedges and is an example of how it should be done.

Above: If you intend to enter an old Beetle in concours d'elegance or classic car shows, then an original and authentic specification is vital. This 1951 split-window model has a later standard of tail-lamps, bumper and engine which no doubt make it a better car but which would be marked down by a concours judge as non-original parts.

usually solve the problem. Failing this, the solenoid could be faulty or the clutch might need replacing. Parts are obtainable and fitment is not difficult. If the clutch snatches or slips, this can be rectified by an adjustment of the vacuum control valve which is to be found on the left-hand side of the engine compartment. There is an adjusting screw which regulates the rate at which the clutch engages and disengages.

The torque converter rarely gives trouble. The level of fluid (ATF), in a tank on the right-hand side of the engine compartment, should be checked. As with any fluid, leaks are possible. The ATF pump is combined with the engine oil pump: a rare but potentially serious fault is a leak between the pumps allowing ATF to mix with the oil, a symptom being a *rise* in level of the engine oil.

Correct tuning of carburettor and ignition is important with the automatic transmission: if the idling speed is wrong, it can cause jerkiness or stalling when a gear is selected.

A semi-auto Beetle in concours condition will command at least as high a price as a manual example; possibly more, in view of its rarity value and special features. In average condition or below, a semi-auto may be cheaper than a manual.

This is because it is perceived, quite wrongly, as being expensive to repair and/or less fun to drive. The semi-automatic transmission is not suitable for use with a modified high-performance engine.

(There was also an earlier two-pedal Beetle, known as Saxomat, produced between 1960 and 1967. This merely had an automatic centrifugal clutch, without a torque converter. Saxomat models are now extremely rare.)

Information about availability of new or secondhand parts, repair procedures and cars for sale can be obtained by joining the Semi-Auto Beetle Register.

3

Production history

The following chronology covers principal development and production landmarks during the Beetle's history, but not every trim detail change or internal modification, of which there have been many thousands. Dates indicate the years in which changes were made. From 1955, all major changes were introduced in August and were associated with the following 'model year'. For example, production of the 1958 model with the larger rear window commenced in August 1957, the last oval-window model having been produced in July 1957.

Before 1955, changes were introduced at any time during the year. The oval-window model replaced the split-window model in March 1953 and the engine was enlarged from 1131cc to 1192cc in January 1954. In the earlier years, some changes may have been introduced intermittently. Data prior to 1949 should be regarded as approximate, as supposedly authoritative sources are not always in exact agreement.

1932
Ferdinand Porsche designed a 'Volksauto' for Zündapp with a water-cooled radial five-cylinder engine of 1200cc and 26bhp, with independent suspension using transverse leaf springs. Three prototypes were built. Zündapp abandoned the project.

1933
Porsche designed a Volksauto for NSU. This had torsion bar suspension but with only a single tube at the front and longitudinally-arranged torsion bars at the rear. The engine was an air-cooled flat

four of 1470cc and 28bhp, designed by Josef Kales. Three prototypes were built. NSU had an arrangement with Fiat at that time to produce only motorcycles, so the project did not go ahead.

1934
Franz Reimspiess designed an air-cooled flat four engine, similar to the NSU engine, but of 985cc and 23bhp, which became the basis of all VW Beetle engines. Ferdinand Porsche presented his proposals for a People's Car to the German government.

1935
The first two prototypes of Porsche's People's Car design were built: a saloon (known as V1) and a convertible (V2). These cars had twin-tube torsion bar front suspension and transverse torsion bars with swing-axle at the rear. Various engines were installed. The saloon had no rear window as such; very restricted rear vision was provided through the engine cooling slots. The doors were rear-hinged, opening from the front.

1936
Three more prototypes, known as the VW3 Series, were built and long-distance trials commenced, using the Reimspiess flat four engine.

1937
Another 30 prototypes (VW30) were built and long distance trials commenced, each car covering some 50,000 miles.

Above: *Early Beetles are characterised by the divided or 'split' rear window and W-shaped pressing on the engine cover. Note also the distinctive tail-lamps and fluted bumper. This is a 1952 model.*

Above: *This 1949 model has been converted to right-hand drive but shows the original style of facia, the rudimentary three-spoked steering wheel which was a feature of the early standard model and the roller accelerator pedal. (The seats are not original.)*

Above: *The 1131cc 25bhp engine. This is a 1953 Beetle; earlier engines had a smaller mushroom-shaped air cleaner.*

Right: *Beetles had semaphore indicators until they were replaced by flashing signals in 1957 (USA) and 1960 (Europe).*

1938

The bodywork was extensively changed to incorporate the split rear window (in two parts, as curved glass was not yet available); this left a smaller area for the engine cooling slots and necessitated a larger fan. Doors were changed to open from the rear (front-hinged) and the front bonnet opening was enlarged. Three cars designated VW303 (one saloon, one sunroof, one convertible) were built to this specification, followed by a batch of approximately 40 (known as VW38 Series) which became the initial production standard for the Beetle. The VW303 cars underwent comparative trials with other makes including DKW and Opel. Prototype Kübelwagens (Type 62) were built, based on the VW38 chassis. The VW38 cars (Type 60) were shown to the public and the press and given the name KdF-Wagen.

1939

Approximately 50 cars (VW39 Series) were built. Three aerodynamic sports coupés with 1100cc 40bhp engines were built for the planned Berlin-Rome race, which never took place. The Type 82 Kübelwagen was designed with improved cross-country capability through increased ground clearance (using gears between the drive shafts and hubs) and a locking differential.

1940

Type 82 Kübelwagen went into production. An amphibious version (Type 128) was tested. This had four-wheel drive, engine enlarged to 1131cc and 25bhp, and a propeller engaged with the end of the crankshaft for propulsion in water. Production commenced of a stationary (industrial) version of the Beetle engine.

1942

A shorter wheelbase version of the amphibian (Type 166) went into production and became known as Schwimmwagen.

1941-1945

Production during this period was mostly Kübelwagen (approx. 50,000 vehicles) and Schwimmwagen (approx. 14,000). Other military variants included the Type 82E (Beetle saloon with Kübelwagen chassis), Type 87 Kommandeurwagen (Beetle saloon with fully opening roof, on 4wd chassis similar to Type 128 amphibian), and Type 155 (Kübelwagen with caterpillar tracks).

Approximately 630 Beetles were produced during the war years. The 1131cc engine went into all types in 1943.

1945

Beetle production officially commenced. Small-numbers of special-bodied Beetles were produced, including post office vans and ambulances.

1946

Beetle production reached 10,000. Soundproofing added to engine compartment. Tyre-size changed from 4.50x16 to 5.00x16.

1947

Front wheel bearings strengthened. Exports to Holland commenced.

1948

Rear wheel bearing sealing improved. Exports to Denmark, Luxembourg, Switzerland, Belgium and Sweden commenced. Total production reached 25,000. The coachbuilding firm of Hebmüller was contracted to produce a two-seater Convertible Beetle.

1949

Double-acting telescopic shock absorbers fitted at the front, in place of single-acting. Gearbox casing material changed to Elektron (magnesium alloy). Rear seat legroom increased; footwells formed in floorpan. Cable bonnet release introduced. Improvements made to intake manifold support, oil filler, trackrod adjustment, brakes, heater control, seats, pedals, paintwork and front axle. Starting handle deleted. Production of De Luxe model (sometimes referred to as Export model) commenced. Features included extra soundproofing, chrome trim on running boards, waistline and bonnet, horn fitted behind grille, easier front seat adjustment and two-spoke steering wheel. First Beetle shipped to USA. Total production reached 50,000. Production of four-seater Karmann Convertible commenced.

1950

Hydraulic brakes introduced, on De Luxe model and Convertible only. Materials for pistons, valves and valve seats improved. Thermostat introduced for engine cooling. Front torsion bars changed to five leaves upper and lower. Door window glass slightly cut away at top corner to provide ventilation. Noise suppression added to heater pipes. Sunroof model introduced. Exports to Brazil and Ireland commenced. First VW importer appointed in USA. Colborne Garage in Ripley, Surrey, obtained import licence for VW spares and commenced servicing VWs in England. Total production reached 100,000. Production of Commercial (Type 2) commenced.

1951

Ventilation flaps added to side panels in front of doors. Crankcase made of Elektron magnesium alloy. Double acting telescopic shock absorbers fitted at the rear, in place of vane type. Assembly of Beetles commenced in South Africa. Beetles exported to 29 countries. Total production reached 250,000.

Above: *These ventilation flaps were unique to the 1951-52 models, being deleted when opening quarter vent windows were introduced in October 1952. Note also the cutaway corner of the window glass which was the earliest attempt to provide ventilation.*

Below: *One of the rarest Beetle derivatives is the two-seater convertible made by Hebmüller. Only a few hundred were produced between 1949 and 1953 while the mass-produced Beetle convertible became the four-seater produced by Karmann. Tail-lamps on this example are not original.*

1952

Opening quarter vent windows introduced; flaps in lower side panel deleted. Dashboard redesigned: speedometer directly in front of driver, large grille for radio in centre, glovebox on passenger side only. Bumper profile changed (flutes deleted). Horn grilles changed from round to oval. Tail lamps reshaped, with heart-shaped lenses on top for brake lights. Front torsion bars changed to six leaves and rear torsion bar diameter reduced from 25mm to 24mm. Syncromesh on second, third and fourth gears, on De Luxe and Convertible only. Carburettor fitted with accelerator pump jet. Valve springs changed from double to single. Windscreen wiper speed increased; self-parking added. Window crank gearing changed to reduce number of turns from 10½ to 3¼. Turn signal switch mounted on steering column. Interior light repositioned. Wheel size changed from 3½-16 to 4-15, tyre size changed to 5.60x15. Colborne Garage obtained licence to import VWs for sale to US servicemen stationed in England.

1953

One-piece oval rear window introduced. Front torsion bars changed to eight leaves. Fuel tank filler enlarged. VW factory established in Brazil. Exports to Australia started. Irishman Stephen O'Flaherty granted franchise to sell VWs in England and founded Volkswagen Motors Ltd in London as UK importers. Total production reached 500,000. Hebmüller production ceased due to bankruptcy after factory fire; only 696 examples had been built.

1954

Cylinder bore increased from 75mm to 77mm, increasing capacity from 1131cc to 1192cc and power output from 25bhp to 30bhp. Inlet valves enlarged, distributor fitted with vacuum and centrifugal advance, compression raised to 6.6 to 1. Combined ignition-starter key switch replaced push-button starter. Assembly of Beetles commenced in Australia.

Previous page
The first significant change to the Beetle sedan was the oval rear window introduced in March 1953. Early 'ovals' still had the 25bhp engine; it was replaced by the 1192cc 30bhp engine at the end of 1953 and in the following year the single tailpipe exhaust was changed to twin tailpipes.

Above: This style of dashboard was introduced in October 1952 and continued throughout the 'oval window' era. The cranked gear lever seen here came in 1955.

Left: The large rectangular fuel tank seriously limited luggage space until it was redesigned in 1955. This 1953 model has the largest (80mm) filler cap.

Right: Tail-lamps with heart-shaped brake lights on top identify 1953-55 models.

Above: *These tail-lamps, which had twin filament bulbs to provide the brake light function, were fitted from 1956 to 1961.*

Below: *In 1960 the power of the 1192cc engine was raised to 34bhp and this engine, practically unchanged, has endured for more than three decades of Beetle production. The main visible changes have been to the air cleaner. This is a 1962 model with long, snake-like preheat pipe.*

Opposite page
The style of facia seen here, which was introduced with the larger rear window in 1957, has also endured on all torsion bar Beetles. On this 1962 model there is a separate fuel gauge next to the speedo; from 1967 the fuel gauge was accommodated within the speedo dial. The 'bud vase' and parcel shelf were popular accessories.

Know The Year

The following is a quick guide to identifying the age of a Beetle from major visible features.

The **split rear window** dates a Beetle as earlier than March 1953. Hydraulic brakes were introduced in 1950 and syncromesh gears (second, third and fourth) in 1952.

The **oval rear window** identifies Beetles made from March 1953 tp July 1957.

The **rectangular rear window** arrived in August 1957.

Flashing turn signals (instead of the semaphore type), together with the 34bhp engine and all-syncro gearbox, were introduced in August 1960.

Larger windows all round, with a sloping quarter vent pillar, identify Beetles made from August 1964.

The **1300 engine** and ball-joint front suspension came in August 1965.

The **1500 engine**, four-bolt wheels, z-bar and disc brakes were introduced in August 1966.

Vertical headlamps and 12-volt electrics, plus the Europa bumpers, were first seen in August 1967.

Double-jointed rear suspension first appeared on the Automatic Beetle in August 1967.

The **1302S** with strut front suspension and 1600 engine went into production in August 1970.

The **1303S** with panoramic front windscreen replaced the 1302S in August 1972.

Front turn signals wwre first installed in the bumper in August 1974.

1303S Beetle production ceased in July 1975 and 1303S Cabriolet production ceased in January 1980.

The last Beetles (1200s) were made in Europe and the last rhd models were sold in Britain in 1978.

The last European-specification 1200 Beetles, made in Mexico, were sold in Germany in 1986.

Above: This was the first type of flashing front turn signal which replaced semaphore indicators in Europe in 1960.

Below: The front turn signal flashers were enlarged in 1963.

1955

Twin tailpipe exhaust replaced single pipe. Petrol tank redesigned to increase luggage space. Gear lever moved forward and cranked; steering wheel spokes lowered. Front seats provided with three-position adjustment of backrest. Tail lamps redesigned and fitted with twin filament bulbs. Volkswagen of America established (total sales in USA prior to this were approximately 9,000). Total production reached one million. Production of Karmann Ghia Coupé commenced. Front anti-roll bar introduced for Karmann Ghia only.

1956

Outside rear view mirror introduced. Tubeless tyres introduced. Starter motor output increased. Alloy camshaft gear replaced fibre gear.

1957

Rear window enlarged by 95% (more rectangular instead of oval) and windscreen enlarged by 15% (taller and with narrower pillars). Dashboard redesigned with loudspeaker grille next to speedometer, larger glovebox and repositioned switches. Flat accelerator pedal replaced roller type. Flashing turn signals introduced for US market only. Total production reached two million. Production of Karmann Ghia Convertible commenced.

1958

No major changes.

1959

Engine and transmission tilted by two degrees to lower the centre of the swing-axle by 15mm. Rear torsion bar diameter reduced to 22mm and length reduced to 552mm. Anti-roll bar fitted to front suspension. Steering wheel restyled and fitted with half horn ring. Push-button door handles introduced. Padded sunvisors introduced. Exhaust joints fitted with asbestos rings and clamps. Oil drain plug repositioned. Footrest added for front passenger. Heelboard panels added beneath rear seat. Volkswagen do Brazil started complete Beetle manufacture.

1960

Power output increased to 34bhp. Crankcase strengthened and crankshaft redesigned, dynamo/fan support made as separate casting (previously integral with crankcase), inlet valves enlarged from 30mm to 31.5mm, exhaust valves enlarged from 28mm to 30mm, compression ratio increased to 7 to 1, carburettor fitted with automatic choke, intake air preheating added, distributor changed to all-vacuum control, cylinder heads redesigned with additional cooling, fuel pump repositioned. Gearbox redesigned with syncromesh added on first gear. Fuel tank changed to 'flat' design for further luggage space. Flashing turn signals replaced semaphores on European cars. Electric system changed to 'push-on' connectors instead of screw type; fuse box repositioned. Speedometer scale extended to 90mph/140kph (previously 80mph/120kph). Headlamps changed to give asymmetric dipped beam. Exports to USA reached 500,000.

Right: *From 1964 the rear seat could be folded down almost flat and secured in this position with a strap to provide extra luggage space.*

Right: *A steel sliding sunroof became available as a factory-fitted option in 1963. Previously the sunroof had been the fabric folding type.*

Below: *The 1500 Beetle with 44bhp was launched in 1966 and advertised as 'the new hot VW'. Another slogan, reflecting the Beetle's famous ability to cope with rough terrain, was 'The Beetle goes where there is no road'.*

Opposite page
Top: *The Karmann Beetle Cabriolet had been in production since 1949. This is a 1968 model with 1500cc engine. The Cabriolet generally had a more de luxe specification than the Beetle saloon. Standard fittings seen here include wheel trims, over-riders, stone-guards and a passenger's door pocket, The Cabrio always had a slotted engine lid as there was no space for air intake slots in the bodywork above. The folded hood restricts visibility to the rear. The cover, or 'hood bag', should always be fitted when driving with the top down.*

Above: *With the 1500cc engine came disc brakes at the front...*

Below: *...and the Z-bar at the rear, which signficantly improved the handling of the swing-axle suspension.*

Above: The Cabriolet's multi-layer top is insulated and fully lined and is regarded as the world's best soft top.

Left: When the top is closed, the Beetle Convertible is just like a saloon inside. All windows are glass, not plastic.

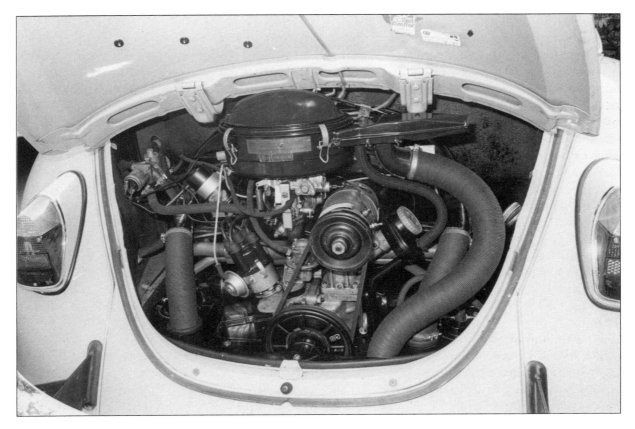

1961

Petrol gauge fitted; reserve tap deleted. Pneumatic screenwasher introduced. Seat belt anchorages built in. Tail lamps redesigned, incorporating separate amber section for turn signals. Sliding covers fitted to heating outlets in front footwells; rear heating outlets in heelboards beneath seat. Type 3 Notchback and Karmann Ghia introduced, powered by 1493cc 45bhp engine. Total production of all Types reached five million.

1962

Vinyl headlining replaced cloth type. Wolfsburg crest on bonnet deleted. Rear heating outlets fitted with regulator. Hydraulic brakes fitted to Standard model. Type 3 Variant (estate car) introduced.

1963

'Fresh air heating' introduced (entered production December 1962) with heat exchangers round exhaust pipes and ducting from each side of fanhousing. Steel sliding sunroof introduced (previous folding fabric sunroof remained available on Standard model until 1967). Front turn signal flashers enlarged. Housing for rear number plate lamp widened. Horn ring deleted;

horn now operated by short bars on the spokes. Type 3 1500S introduced with twin-carb high-compression engine giving 54bhp.

1964

Windows enlarged; windscreen very slightly curved and height increased by 28mm; rear window extended by 20mm and side windows given slimmer frames. Pillar between quarter vent and door window inclined. Heater controlled by two levers instead of rotary knob. Push-button release for engine lid, in place of T-shaped handle. All-syncro gearbox fitted to Standard model. Engine cooling air regulated by flaps on outlet side of fan instead of throttle ring on inlet side. Distributor modified to retard timing of number 3 cylinder.

1965

1300 Beetle introduced with 1285cc engine giving 40bhp (stroke increased from 64mm to 69mm using the crankshaft from the '1500' Type 3), inlet valves enlarged to 33mm, larger carburettor fitted (Solex 30 PICT), compression raised to 7.3 to 1. Front axle redesigned using ball-joints instead of link pins. Dimension between torsion bar tubes increased from 120mm to 150mm, torsion bars changed to 10 leaves, upper ball-joint fitted with eccentric bush for camber adjustment. Seat backrests provided with locking mechanism. Third demister slot added in centre of facia. Horn reverted to half ring as in 1962. Slotted wheels introduced, with flatter hubcaps. Dipswitch operated by button on turn signal lever on steering column instead of foot switch. Copper core ignition leads replaced resistor leads. Suppressor plug caps fitted. Accelerator pedal given progressive action by means of roller running along a curved plate. Manufacture of Beetles commenced in Mexico. Type 3 Fastback introduced, known as 1600TL. Engine size of Type 3 models enlarged to 1584cc, giving 54bhp. Production commenced of small Beetle-based delivery van, known as VW 147 or 'Fridolin', primarily for post office use.

1966

1500 Beetle introduced with 1493cc engine giving 44bhp (bore increased from 77mm to 83mm), inlet valves enlarged to 35.5mm, exhaust valves enlarged to 32mm, compression raised to 7.5 to 1. Rear suspension fitted with 'equaliser spring', better known as 'Z-bar' because of its shape which gave the opposite effect to that of a U-shaped anti-roll bar. Rear torsion bar diameter reduced to 21mm. Rear track widened from 50.7in to 53.1in. Front disc brakes introduced (1500 only), together with four-bolt wheels instead of five-bolt. Dynamo 'cut-in' speed reduced. Regulator repositioned under rear seat. Flywheel diameter increased. Number of teeth on starter ring gear changed from 109 to 130. Dashboard knobs changed to larger soft plastic to prevent injury. Door locks operated by button in rear corner of window frame.

Previous page
The engine of a 1969 1500 Automatic Beetle. The auto stick-shift transmission has an electro-pneumatic clutch, the control unit of which is located at the top left of the engine compartment. Also just visible, behind the preheat hose on the right, is the filler for the torque converter fluid.

Right: Double-jointed rear suspension was first fitted to Beetles with automatic transmission, in 1967. It then became standard for all Beetles for the USA and was subsequently a feature of the 1302 and 1303.

1967

1300 and 1500 Beetles (but not 1200) fitted with 12-volt electrical system, vertical headlamps, enlarged tail lamps, larger and stronger bumpers, fresh air ventilation and dual circuit brakes. Safety features included collapsible steering column, trigger-type door handles, 'break-away' interior mirror and mountings for rear seat belts. Fuel tank filler repositioned behind flap for external access. Fuel gauge incorporated in speedometer dial. Exterior mirror enlarged. Gear lever shortened and moved closer to seat. Two-speed wipers fitted. Padded dashboard and reversing lights available as options. Semi-automatic Beetle introduced, featuring double-jointed rear suspension. Total Beetle production reached ten million.

1968

Double-jointed rear suspension fitted to Beetles with manual transmission for USA. Fuel filler cap fitted with lock and cable release. Bonnet release located inside glovebox. Hazard warning flashers introduced. Radial tyres standard for UK market (except 1200). Production of Type 4 Saloon (VW 411) commenced, powered by all-new 1679cc 68bhp engine.

1969

Oil system modified; crankcase fitted with two oil pressure control valves. Extra air intake slots in engine cover on 1500 Beetle. Dual circuit brakes fitted to 1200 Beetle. VW 181 multi-purpose vehicle introduced.

Opposite page
Top, left: *An external fuel filler was first seen on 1968 models, but it was not fitted with a lock until the following year. The Beetle has always been able to run on low-octane petrol — the sticker states that 87 octane is the minimum.*

Top, right: *The locking fuel filler cap had a cable release operated by a pull-handle beneath the facia. With the introduction of the 1303 this was deleted in favour of an optional key-locking cap.*

Bottom, right: *For many years Beetles had a pneumatic screenwasher which could be connected to the spare tyre to maintain pressure. Only recent Mexican-built Beetles have an electric screenwasher.*

Above: *High-backed seats were part of the safety package for the US market in 1968. The safety aspect of restricted visibility was questionable!*

Below: *The Beetle was one of the first European small cars to have hazard warning flashers as standard. The switch was located beneath the radio and fresh air controls.*

1970

New model 1302S introduced, features including MacPherson strut front suspension with coil springs and semi-trailing arm double-jointed rear suspension, enlarged luggage capacity and 1584cc engine with 50bhp. Both this and the 1300 engine had new cylinder heads with twin inlet ports, new crankcase (AS-41 alloy), a wider fan and repositioned oil cooler giving improved cooling air flow to number 3 cylinder. Through-flow ventilation, with crescent-shaped outlets behind rear side windows, fitted to both 1300 and 1302/1302S. Power output of 1300 engine increased to 44bhp. Engine cover provided with cooling slots, as previously on 1500. Headlamps switched off with ignition.

1971

Slots in engine cover increased from 10 to 26, water drainage tray beneath slots deleted, electrical components provided with greater protection against rain. Rear window height increased by 40mm. Four-spoke steering wheel introduced, with switch lever for windscreen wipers on column. Removable cover fitted to rear luggage compartment (not 1200). Distributor changed to single vacuum control. Computer diagnosis introduced. Total VW exports to USA reached five million.

1972

New model 1303/1303S introduced, replacing 1302/1302S. Features included larger and more curved 'panoramic' windscreen, completely redesigned all-padded dashboard, improved ventilation and defrosting, new three-point mountings for front seats and large 'elephant's foot' rear lamps. The 1303S was powered by the 1600cc/50bhp engine and the 1303 by the 1300/44 engine. (It was also available in Germany with the 1200/34 engine.) The torsion bar chassis 1200 and 1300 Beetles continued in production. The Convertible was based on the 1303S. In February 1972 Beetle production reached 15,007,034, thereby beating the previous production record held by the Model T Ford. This feat was commemorated by a special edition 'World Champion' or 'Marathon' 1300 Beetle. The 1600cc/50bhp engine became available in the torsion bar/swing-axle chassis (with disc brakes), this model being designated 1300S. It was available in the UK from December 1972, known as GT Beetle.

1973

All Beetles with coil spring strut front suspension fitted with Audi 80-type negative offset steering geometry ('self-stabilising' steering). 1200 Beetles fitted with large rear lamps as on 1303. Various limited editions with special trim introduced, including the 'Yellow and Black Racer' and the 'Big Beetle' which were fitted with 5½-15 sports wheels and 175/70x15 tyres. 1200L introduced with improved equipment level.

1974

Front turn signals fitted in bumper instead of on top of wings. Rack and pinion steering fitted to 1303 models. Fuel injection and catalytic converter introduced for USA. 1303S omitted from UK model range. Brazilian production included twin-carb Super Fusca. Domestic production ceased at Wolfsburg in July 1974 but continued at Emden.

Above: The 1970 single-port 1500 (left)and 1971 twin-port 1300 both produced 44bhp, but the 1500 gave more torque.Both had two rows of cooling slots in the engine lid. The '71 model had through-flow ventilation, the outlets for which are the crescent-shaped slots behind the side window. This style of tail-lamp and 'Europa' bumper was introduced in 1967.

Opposite page
Comparison of a torsion bar Beetle (Peter Noad's 1970 model 1500) with a McPherson strut 1302S. The latter has a longer, more bulbous bonnet.

1975

Production of 1303 and 1303S terminated, except Convertible. Basic 1200 Beetle available with either 1200cc/34bhp engine or 1600/50 engine, the latter together with disc brakes, Z-bar and slotted engine cover. Production of the 1300/44 engine ceased. 1200 Beetle fitted with 12-volt electrical system. 1200L fitted with two-speed ventilation fan. Assembly of Beetles commenced in Nigeria. Only model available in UK was 34bhp 1200L.

1976

No change. UK range comprised 1200L and 1303S Convertible.

1977

No change. Special 'Champagne Edition' Convertible produced for USA.

1978

European production terminated. except of Convertible. 1200L imported from Mexico and sold in Germany. Mexican-built Beetle differed from recent European versions: smaller (pre-1971) rear window, 34bhp engine only, dynamo instead of alternator, ventilation fan omitted, Z-bar and head restraints fitted. South African Beetle production included 1600 SP with twin-carb 58bhp engine and extra instruments. Special batch of 600 Emden-built Beetles sold in UK as the 'Last Edition'. 300 of these, with silver paintwork, had a serial-numbered 'Last Edition' plaque.

1979

No change. Brazilian production included a Beetle running on alcohol fuel.

1980

No change. Production of the Convertible ceased in January 1980, having reached a total of 332,000.

1981

Total Beetle production reached 20 million. To mark this achievement, a limited edition 'Silver Bug' was produced, its features including special paintwork and interior trim and special '20 Million' plaques. Slots in engine cover deleted.

1982

Electric screenwasher replaced pneumatic type. Limited editions produced with special trim: 'Jeans Bug' and 'Special Bug'.

1983
No change. Limited editions with special trim: 'Aubergine Beetle' and 'Metallic Ice Blue Beetle'.

1984
No change. More limited editions with special trim: 'Sunny Bug' and 'Velvet Red Beetle'.

1985
Import of Mexican Beetles to Germany terminated. Special edition 'Jubilee Beetle' produced to celebrate the Beetle's 50th anniversary, with special paintwork and trim and '50 Jahre Käfer' badge.

1986.
Beetle production in Brazil terminated.

1987-1990
Beetle production continued in Mexico, with specification reduced to maintain low price. Government tax concessions in Mexico resulted in increased demand. Production increased to more than 400 per day. Electronic ignition and anti-theft alarm fitted. Fresh air ventilation, rear heater outlets, rear seat belts, undersealing and dual circuit for braking system deleted. 1200 and 1600 engines produced, the latter with low compression giving 44bhp.

1991
Unregulated two-way catalyst fitted.

1992
Rear seat belt mountings and full dual circuit brakes reinstated. Total production reached 21 million. Major engine changes announced for the 1993 model year including Digifant fuel injection, hydraulic tappets, 'proper' oil filtration and regulated three-way catalyst.

1993
Production recommenced in Brazil.

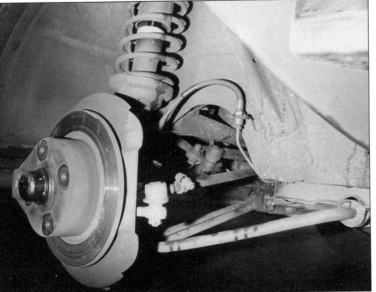

Left: With the change from torsion bar to strut front suspension there was a substantial increase in luggage capacity.

Left: The strut suspension was similar to that commonly used on front-engined cars. The anti-roll bar also serves as a track control arm. Only the 1600-engined European models (1302S and 1303S) had disc brakes. The 1300-engined 1302 and 1303, and all USA-market cars, retained drum brakes all round.

Opposite page
Top: The first right-hand-drive padded dash was seen on the 1302S in 1972. This four-spoke steering wheel became standard for Beetles.

Bottom: As seen in this comparison of a 1302S and 1500, the strut suspension provided more steering lock and a tighter turning circle. While radial tyres were standard on the 1970 1500 (UK market), the 1302S reverted to crossply tyres in 1971.

Above: The fully slotted engine lid necessitated some degree of waterproofing of the electrics: note the caps on the dynamo terminals. In 1972 the oil bath air cleaner had vacuum and temperature connections to provide complex control of preheating, but this was not entirely successful in eliminating the acceleration flat spots that afflicted the twin-port engines with stricter exhaust emission controls.

Left: Beetles were originally manufactured in Brazil from 1959 to 1986. Specifications often differed from European-made Beetles, one reason being that older standards of tooling were used in the Brazilian factory. This example has the small window pre-1965 bodyshell with post-1970 through-flow ventilation and the 1973 tail-lamps. This type of wheel is unique to Brazilian Beetles.

Below: One of the most desirable Beetles is the GT Beetle, sold as a special edition in the UK in 1973. 'GT Beetle' badging was purely for the British market: elsewhere in Europe this model was the 1300S.

Right: The last phase in the evolution of the Beetle before European production ceased was the curved windscreen model, designated 1303 or 1303S. The 1303 saloon was only made from August 1972 to July 1975, but the '03' continued as a Cabriolet until January 1980.

Below: The last mechanical change was the introduction of rack and pinion steering and Audi 80-type negative offset steering geometry, found only on the 1303 and 1303S.

Right: The final batch of righthand-drive Beetles, sold in Britain in 1978, were 1200L models known as the Last Edition. There were 300 of them, finished in Diamond Silver metallic paint, with commemorative serial-numbered dashboard plaques.

Above: *Fuel injection was introduced for the American market in 1974 and is commonly found on left-hand-drive 1303 Cabriolets which have been imported into Britain. Many also have air-conditioning, as seen here.*

Left: *Mexican-built 1200 Beetles continued to be sold in Europe until early 1986. The last batch, known as Jubilee Beetles, had special badges commemorating 50 years of Beetles since the first prototypes were built in Germany in 1935.*

Below: *A 1994 Mexican Beetle engine with fuel injection, electronic ignition, hydraulic tappets and a 'proper' oil filter. (Air filter and exhaust system are not fitted in this picture.) The power output of 46bhp remains the same as previous Mexican 1.6-litre Beetle engines.*

4

Facts and figures

Chassis Numbers

The Beetle has always had the factory designation of Type 1 and, with the exception of the period from 1956 to 1964, the chassis numbers have a 1 or 11 prefix to denote the vehicle type.

Type 1 chassis numbers commenced at 1-00001 in 1940, but during the war years Type 1 included the military derivatives (eg Kübelwagen), so the chassis number sequence was not a count of Beetle production. Only a few hundred Beetle saloons had been built when the chassis numbering reached 1-053814 in December 1945.

In 1955 production reached one million, necessitating the use of seven digits following the Type 1 prefix. The last car produced in 1955 was numbered 1-1060929. The prefix was then dropped and the last car produced in 1956 was number 1394119. Production reached six million in 1964 and the last 1964 model, produced in July of that year, was number 6502399.

Commencing with the first 1965 model, produced in August 1964, there was a new numbering system with a three-digit prefix consisting of 11 to denote the Beetle saloon (by this time the Karmann Ghia had been designated Type 14 and the Convertible Type 15), followed by a digit to denote the model year, eg 5 for 1965. The first Beetle off the line in August 1964 was therefore 115 000 001, the first 1966 Beetle in August 1965 was 116 000 001, and so on.

Obviously this sytem would lead to duplication in 1974, so commencing in 1970 a 2 was inserted to indicate the second decade. Thus, the first 1970 model produced in August 1969 was 110 2 000 001. (Note: 1 had already appeared as the fourth digit when production exceeded one million in a single year.)

This system continued until the end of the decade. The last Beetle saloon manufactured in Germany was 118 2 034 030. The 1303 Beetle was given the prefix 13.

Instead of progressing to 110 3 as the prefix for the next decade, the first 1980 model, produced in August 1979, was given the chassis number 11A 0000001. With the introduction of the international standardised vehicle identification number (VIN), this became WVWzzz11zAM 000001.

WVW is the manufactirer's code for Volkswagen private cars. The z's are fill-in characters or blanks. The letter M in the 11th position denotes the country of manufacture, in this case Mexico.

This system of chassis numbering continues, with the year letter moving through the alphabet, but omitting I and O. The first 1993 model Beetle was 11 PM000001.

Type Numbers

As mentioned above, the Beetle was designated Type 1, with variations such as the Karmann Ghia, Convertible and 1303 identified by a second digit. Only the first two 'Type' digits are used in the chassis number. The full Type number was originally made up of three digits and then, from 1968, six digits.

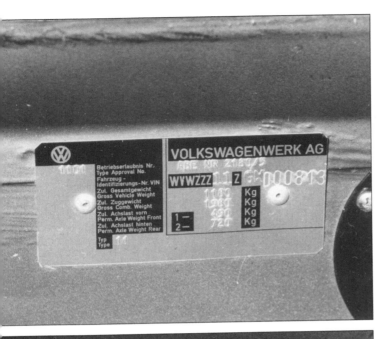

Left: *The vehicle identification plate, found behind the spare wheel, shows the type approval number, chassis number, and permitted weights.*

Left, below: *The chassis number (WVW GM000813) also appears on a sticker in the spare wheel compartment together with the VW type number (111 211), engine code letter (D), gearbox code (AB), paint code (LA7Y) and option codes. The last-named includes factory-fitted options such as heated rear window.*

Below: *The chassis number is also stamped on the central tunnel of the floorpan underneath the rear seat.*

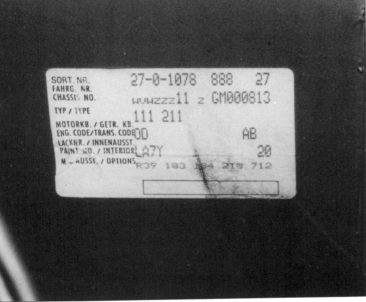

Prior to the introduction of the 34bhp engine in August 1960, the allocation of Type numbers was as follows:

111	Standard saloon, left-hand drive
112	Standard saloon, right-hand drive
113	Export saloon, left-hand drive
114	Export saloon, right-hand drive
115	Standard saloon with sun-roof, left-hand drive
116	Standard Saloon with sun-roof, right-hand drive
117	Export saloon with sun-roof, left-hand drive
118	Export saloon with sun-roof, right-hand drive.

From 1960 the 'Standard' Type numbers were associated with the 30bhp engine and the 'Export' type numbers denoted the 34bhp engine.

When the 1300 and 1500 engines were introduced, Types 111, 112, 115 and 116 were used for the 1200 and Types 113, 114, 117 and 118 for the 1300 and 1500.

In 1968 three more digits were added to the Type number and the six digits were used as follows:

1st digit 1 = Beetle
2nd digit 1 = 1200/1300/1500
2 = Industrial engine applications
3 = 1303
4 = Karmann Ghia
5 = Convertible
6 = Multi-purpose vehicle
(eg Trekker or Thing)
3rd digit 1,3,5 = Left-hand drive
2,4,6 = Right-hand drive
4th digit 0 = Normal model
1 = 'L' version
7,8 = USA versions
5th digit Engine type:
1 = 1200 34bhp
2 = 1300 44bhp
3 = 1500 44bhp or 1600 50bhp
4 = 1500 with emission control
5 = 1600 48bhp
6 = 1600 48bhp
*For absolute engine definitions,
see 'Engine Codes', below.*
6th digit 1 = Manual gearbox
2 = Automatic transmission

Thus, for example, a right-hand-drive 1500 Automatic would be numbered 114032 and a left-hand-drive 1303L Manual 135121.

Engine Codes

Engine code letters, as a prefix to the engine number, were first used in 1965 with the introduction of the 1300. Those applicable to Beetle engines are as follows:

A	1200 30bhp
D	1200 34bhp
E	1300 37bhp (low compression)
F	1300 40bhp
H	1500 44bhp
L	1500 40bhp (low compression)
AB	1300 44bhp
AC	1300 40bhp (low compression)
AD	1600 50bhp
AE	1600 48bhp (USA)
AF	1600 46bhp (low compression)
AG	1600 44bhp (Type 181)
AH	1600 48bhp (USA)
AJ	1600 50bhp (fuel injection)
AK	1600 48bhp (USA)
AL	1600 48bhp (Type 181)
AM	1600 48bhp (Type 181, USA)
AR	1300 44bhp
AS	1600 50bhp

Above: The engine number (D1 534697) is stamped on the crankcase just above the crankshaft pulley. The words 'Hecho en Mexico' in the casting beneath the distributor indicate that this is a Mexican-built engine.

Specifications and Performance

There have been countless variations of the Beetle's specification for different markets all over the world. These include low-compression engines for countries with very low-grade fuel, engines with extra emission control for areas such as California, high-performance twin-carburettor models produced in Brazil and South Africa, fuel injection for the USA, double-jointed rear suspension with torsion bar front suspension and manual gearbox for the USA, and German-market permutations such as a 1200 engine in the 1303 body and 1600 engine in the 1200 body. Derivatives such as the Karmann Ghia and Type 181 were mechanically very similar to the Beetle, but differed in terms of weight, gear ratios and performance.

The following specifications and data cover the best-known models which were available in Britain (though not exclusively in Britain, of course).

Despite a consistent commonality of many specifications, we have given figures for each model in full, rather than adopt the 'same as... except for' approach which involves the reader in tiresome cross-referring.

Performance figures for pre-1960 models are from road tests published in *Autocar* magazine. All other performance figures are from the author's own road tests.

1200
(UP TO DECEMBER 1953)

Above: 1200 up to 1953

Engine type: Rear-mounted, horizontally opposed four-cylinder, air-cooled, with two pushrod-operated overhead valves per cylinder. Aluminium alloy cylinder heads (one per pair of cylinders), cast-iron cylinder barrels, magnesium alloy crankcase with four-bearing crankshaft.

Bore: 75mm
Stroke: 64mm
Capacity: 1131cc
Compression ratio: 5.8 to 1
Fuel system: Solex 28 PCI carburettor (Solex 26 VFJ before 10/52), oil bath air cleaner (felt type before 1/53), mechanical fuel pump.
Power: 25bhp at 3300rpm
Torque: 51 lb ft at 2000rpm
Transmission: Four-speed manual gearbox. Export model: syncromesh on second, third and fourth, ratios — 1st 3.60, 2nd 1.88, 3rd 1.23, 4th 0.79, reverse 4.63. Standard model: non-syncromesh, ratios — 1st 3.60, 2nd 2.07, 3rd 1.25, 4th 0.80, reverse 6.60. Final drive ratio 4.43. Cable-operated single-plate clutch.
Suspension: Independent front suspension with transverse laminated torsion bars and trailing arms, telescopic shock absorbers. Independent rear suspension with swing axles, transverse torsion bars and trailing arms, telescopic shock absorbers (lever arm vane type before 1951).
Steering: Worm and sector, 2.4 turns lock to lock.
Brakes: Front drums 230mm dia. x 30mm wide, rear drums 230mm x 30mm. Export model: hydraulic operation. Standard model: mechanical operation.
Wheels and Tyres: Steel disc wheels with five-bolt fixing, 4J-15, with 5.60-15 crossply tyres (3.5D-16 with 5.00-16 tyres before 10/52).
Length: 4070mm (160in)
Width: 1540mm (60.6in)
Height: 1500mm (59in)
Wheelbase: 2400mm (94.5in)
Unladen weight: 730kg (1610lb)
Typical Performance: Maximum speed 63mph, 0-50mph 24.3sec, average fuel consumption 37mpg.

1200
(JANUARY 1954-JULY 1960 EXPORT MODEL; TO JULY 1965 STANDARD MODEL)

Engine type: Rear-mounted, horizontally opposed four-cylinder, air-cooled, with two pushrod-operated overhead valves per cylinder. Aluminium alloy cylinder heads (one per pair of cylinders), cast-iron cylinder barrels, magnesium alloy crankcase with four-bearing crankshaft.

Bore: 77mm
Stroke: 64mm
Capacity: 1192cc
Compression ratio: 6.6 to 1 (6.1 to 1 before 8/53)
Fuel system: Solex 28 PCI carburettor, oil bath air cleaner, mechanical fuel pump.
Power: 30bhp at 3400rpm
Torque: 56 lb ft at 2000rpm
Transmission: Four-speed manual gearbox. Export model: syncromesh on second, third and fourth, ratios — 1st 3.60, 2nd 1.88, 3rd 1.23, 4th 0.82, reverse 4.63. Standard model: non-syncromesh, ratios — 1st 3.60, 2nd 2.07, 3rd 1.25, 4th 0.80, reverse 6.60. Final drive ratio 4.43. Cable-operated single-plate clutch.

Suspension: Independent front suspension with transverse laminated torsion bars and trailing arms, telescopic shock absorbers. Independent rear suspension with swing axles, transverse torsion bars and trailing arms, telescopic shock absorbers.
Steering: Worm and sector, 2.4 turns lock to lock.
Brakes: Front drums 230mm x 40mm (230mm x 30mm on Standard model and before 10/57 on Export model), rear drums 230mm x 30mm. Export model: hydraulic operation. Standard model: mechanical operation.
Wheels and Tyres: Steel disc wheels with five-bolt fixing, 4J-15, with 5.60-15 crossply tyres.
Length: 4070mm (160in)
Width: 1540mm (60.6in)
Height: 1500mm (59in)
Wheelbase: 2400mm (94.5in)
Unladen weight: 730kg (1610lb)
Typical Performance: Maximum speed 68mph, 0-50mph 18.2sec, 0-60mph 32.4sec, average fuel consumption 31mpg.

Below: 1200 1954-1960

Left: 1200 1960 on

Below: 1300 1965-1970

Opposite page:
Top: 1500

Bottom: 1500 Automatic

1200
(FROM AUGUST 1960, EXPORT MODEL)

Engine type: Rear-mounted, horizontally opposed four-cylinder, air-cooled, with two
pushrod-operated overhead valves per cylinder.
Aluminium alloy cxylinder heads (one per pair of
cylinders), cast-iron cylinder barrels, magnesium
alloy crankcase with four-bearing crankshaft.

Bore: 77mm
Stroke: 64mm
Capacity: 1192cc
Compression: 7.0 to 1 (7.3 to 1 from 8/72)
Fuel system: Solex 28 PICT carburettor (30
PICT from 8/70), oil bath air cleaner (paper
element from 8/75), mechanical fuel pump.
Power: 34bhp at 3600rpm (3800rpm from
8/72)
Torque: 61 lb ft at 2000rpm (55 lb ft at 1700rpm
from 8/72)

Transmission: Four-speed manual gearbox,
syncromesh on all forward gears, ratios — 1st
3.80 (3.78 from 11/72), 2nd 2.06, 3rd 1.26 (1.32
nefore 8/66), 4th 0.89 (0.88 from 3/70, 0.93
from 11/72), reverse 3.88 (3.61 from 8/67).
Final drive ratio 4.375. Cable-operated single-
plate clutch.
Suspension: Independent front suspension
with transverse laminated torsion bars and
trailing arms, anti-roll bar and telescopic
shock absorbers. Independent rear suspension
with swing axles, transverse torsion bars and
trailing arms, telescopic shock absorbers.
Z-bar (equaliser spring) fitted from 8/78.
Steering: Worm and roller, 2.6 turns lock to
lock (worm and sector before 8/61).
Brakes: Front drums 230mm x 40mm, rear
drums 230mm x 30mm (230mm x 40mm from
8/67). Hydraulic operation with dual circuit
from 8/69.
Wheels and Tyres: Steel disc wheels with five
bolt fixing (four-bolt from 8/67), 4J-15 (4½J-15
from 2/72), 5.60-15 crossply or 155-15 radial
ply tyres.
Length: 4070mm (160in); 4060mm (159.8in)
from 8/73.
Width: 1540mm (60.6in)
Height: 1500mm
Wheelbase: 2400mm (94.5in)
Unladen weight: 740kg (1631lb) increasing to
780kg (1719lb) by 1976.
Typical Performance: Maximum speed
72mph, 0-50mph 16.9sec, 0-60mph 25.7sec,
average fuel consumption 34mpg

1300
(AUGUST 1965-JULY 1970)

Engine type: Rear-mounted, horizontally opposed four-cylinder, air-cooled, with two pushrod-operated overhead valves per cylinder. Aluminium alloy cylinder heads (one per pair of cylinders), cast-iron cylinder barrels, magnesium alloy crankcase with four-bearing crankshaft.

Bore: 77mm
Stroke: 69mm
Capacity: 1285cc
Compression ratio: 7.3 to 1
Fuel system: Solex 30 PICT carburettor, oil bath air cleaner, mechanical fuel pump.
Power: 40bhp at 4000rpm
Torque: 65.4 lb ft at 2000rpm
Transmission: Four-speed manual gearbox, syncromesh on all forward gears, ratios — 1st 3.80, 2nd 2.06, 3rd 1.26 (1.32 before 8/66), 4th 0.89, reverse 3.61 (3.88 before 8/67). Final drive ratio 4.375. Cable-operated single-plate clutch.
Suspension: Independent front suspension with transverse laminated torsion bars and trailing arms, anti-roll bar and telescopic shock absorbers. Independent rear suspension with swing axles, transverse torsion bars and trailing arms, Z-bar and telescopic shock absorbers.
Steering: Worm and roller, 2.6 turns lock to lock.

Brakes: Front drums 230mm x 40mm, rear drums 230mm x 30mm (230mm x 40mm from 8/67). Hydraulic operation with dual circuit from 8/67.
Wheels and Tyres: Steel disc wheels with four-bolt fixing (five-bolt before 8/67), 4J-15, 5.60-15 crossply or 155-15 radial ply tyres.
Length: 4070mm (160in); 4060mm (159.8in) from 8/67.
Width: 1540mm (60.6in)
Height: 1500mm (59in)
Wheelbase: 2400mm (94.5in)
Unladen weight: 820kg (1808lb)
Typical Performance: Maximum speed 75mph, 0-50mph 13.6sec, 0-60mph 20.5sec, 0-70mph 35.5sec, average fuel consumption 35mpg.

1500
(AUGUST 1966-JULY 1970)

Engine type: Rear-mounted, horizontally opposed four-cylinder, air-cooled, with two pushrod-operated valves per cylinder. Aluminium alloy cylinder heads (one per pair of cylinders), cast-iron cylinder barrels, magnesium alloy crankcase with four-bearing crankshaft.

Bore: 83mm
Stroke: 69mm
Capacity: 1493cc
Compression ratio: 7.5 to 1
Fuel System: Solex 30 PICT carburettor, oil bath cleaner, mechanical fuel pump.
Power: 44bhp at 4000rpm
Torque: 74 lb ft at 2000rpm
Transmission: Four-speed manual gearbox, syncromesh on all forward gears, ratios — 1st 3.80, 2nd 2.06, 3rd 1.26, 4th 0.89, reverse 3.61. Final drive ratio 4.125. Cable-operated single-plate clutch.

Suspension: Independent front suspension with transverse laminated torsion bars and trailing arms, anti-roll bar and telescopic shock absorbers. Independent rear suspension with swing axles, transverse torsion bars and trailing arms, Z-bar and telescopic shock absorbers.
Steering: Worm and roller, 2.6 turns lock to lock.
Brakes: Front discs 277mm dia., rear drums 230mm x 40mm. Hydraulic operation with dual circuit from 8/67.
Wheels and Tyres: Steel disc wheels with four-bolt fixing, 4J-15, 5.60-15 crossply or 155-55 radial ply tyres.
Length: 4060mm (159.8in)
Width: 1540mm (60.6in)
Height: 1500mm (59in)
Wheelbase: 2400mm (94.5in)
Unladen weight: 820kg (1808lb)
Typical Performance: Maximum speed 78mph, 0-50mph 11.3sec, 0-60mph 16.9sec, 0-70mph 26.8sec, average fuel consumption 30mpg

Below: 1300 1971-1975

Above: 1302S

1500
AUTOMATIC (AUGUST 1967-JULY 1970)

Engine type: Rear-mounted, horizontally opposed four-cylinder, air-cooled, with two pushrod-operated valves per cylinder. Aluminium alloy cylinder heads (one per pair of cylinders), cast-iron cylinder barrels, magnesium alloy crankcase with four-bearing crankshaft.

Bore: 83mm

Stroke: 69mm

Capacity: 1493cc

Compression ratio: 7.5 to 1

Fuel system: Solex 30 PICT carburettor, oil bath air cleaner, mechanical fuel pump.

Power: 44bhp at 4000rpm

Torque: 74 lb ft at 2000rpm

Transmission: Three-speed selector automatic, ratios — 1st 2.06, 2nd 1.26, 3rd 0.89, reverse 3.07. Final drive ratio 4.375. Torque converter and electro-pneumatic clutch.

Suspension: Independent front suspension with transverse laminated torsion bars and trailing arms, anti-roll bar and telescopic shock absorbers. Independent rear suspension with double-jointed drive shafts, semi-trailing arms, and transverse torsion bars, telescopic shock absorbers.

Steering: Worm and roller, 2.6 turns lock to lock.

Brakes: Front discs 277mm dia., rear drums 230mm x 40mm. Hydraulic operation with dual circuit.

Wheels and Tyres: Steel disc wheels with four-bolt fixing, 4J-15, 5.60-15 crossply or 155.15 radial ply tyres.

Length: 4060mm (159.8in)

Width: 1540mm (60.6in)

Height: 1500mm (59in)

Wheelbase: 2400mm (94.5in)

Unladen weight: 820kg (1808lb)

Typical Performance: Maximum speed 75mph, 0-50mph 14.3sec, 0-60mph 21.0sec, 0-70mph 40.0sec, average fuel consumption 30mpg.

Above: 1303

1300
(AUGUST 1970-JULY 1975)

Engine type: Rear-mounted, horizontally opposed, air-cooled, with two pushrod-operated valves per cylinder. Aluminium alloy cylinder heads (one per pair of cylinders), cast-iron cylinder barrels, magnesium alloy crankcase with four-bearing crankshaft.

Bore: 77mm
Stroke: 69mm
Capacity: 1285cc
Compression ratio: 7.5 to 1
Fuel system: Solex 31 PICT carburettor, oil bath air cleaner (paper element air cleaner from 8/72), mechanical fuel pump.
Power: 44bhp at 4100rpm
Torque: 64.7 lb ft at 3000rpm
Transmission: Four-speed manual gearbox, syncromesh on all forward gears, ratios — 1st 3.80 (3.78 from 11/72), 2nd 2.06, 3rd 1.26, 4th 0.88 (0.93 from 11/72), reverse 3.61 (3.79 from 2/72). Final drive ratio 4.375. Cable operated single-plate clutch.
Suspension: Independent front suspension with transverse laminated torsion bars and trailing arms, anti-roll bar and telescopic shock absorbers. Independent rear suspension with swing axles, transverse torsion bars and trailing arms, Z-bar and telescopic shock absorbers.
Steering: Worm and roller, 2.6 turns lock to lock.
Brakes: Front drums 230mm x 40mm, rear drums 230mm x 40mm. Hydraulic operation with dual circuit.
Wheels and Tyres: Steel disc wheels with four-bolt fixing, 4J-15 (4½J-15 from 2/72), 5.60-15 crossply or 155-15 radial ply tyres.
Length: 4060mm (159.8in)
Width: 1540mm (60.6in)
Height: 1500mm (59in)
Wheelbase: 2400 (94.5in)
Unladen weight: 820kg (1808lb)
Typical Performance: Maximum speed 78mph, 0-50mph 14.1sec, 0-60mph 20.5sec, 0-70mph 34.0sec, average fuel consumption 31mpg.

1302S
(AUGUST 1970-JULY 1972)

Engine type: Rear-mounted horizontally opposed four-cylinder, air-cooled, with two pushrod-operated overhead valves per cylinder. Aluminium alloy cylinder heads (one per pair of cylinders), cast-iron cylinder barrels, magnesium alloy crankcase with four-bearing crankshaft.

Bore: 85.5mm
Stroke: 69mm
Capacity: 1584cc
Compression ratio: 7.5 to 1
Fuel system: Solex 34 PICT carburettor, oil bath air cleaner, mechanical fuel pump.
Power: 50bhp at 4000rpm
Torque: 79 lb ft at 2800rpm
Transmission: Four-speed manual gearbox, syncromesh on all forward gears, ratios — 1st 3.80, 2nd 2.06, 3rd 1.26, 4th 0.88, reverse 3.61. Final drive ratio 4.125. Cable-operated single-plate clutch.
Suspension: Independent suspension with MacPherson coil spring struts, track control arms and anti-roll bar. Independent rear suspension with double-jointed drive shafts, semi-trailing arms and transverse torsion bars, telescopic shock absorbers.
Steering: Worm and roller, 2.6 turns lock to lock.
Brakes: Front discs, 277mm dia., rear drums 230mm x 40mm. Hydraulic operation with dual circuit.
Wheels and Tyres: Steel disc wheels with four-bolt fixing, 4J-15 (4½J from 2/72), 5.60-15 crossply or 155-15 radial ply tyres.
Length: 4080mm (160.6in)
Width: 1585mm (62.4in)
Height: 1500mm (59in)
Wheelbase: 2420mm (95.3in)
Unladen weight: 870kg (1918lb)
Typical Performance: Maximum speed 81mph, 0-50mph 11.4sec, 0-60mph 16.8sec, 0-70mph 26.4sec, average fuel consumption 25mpg.

1303
(AUGUST 1972-JULY 1975)

Engine type: Rear-mounted, horizontally opposed four-cylinder, air-cooled with two pushrod-operated valves per cylinder. Aluminium alloy cylinder heads (one per pair of cylinders), cast-iron cylinder barrels, magnesium alloy crankcase with four-bearing crankshaft.

Bore: 77mm
Stroke: 69mm
Capacity: 1285cc
Compression ratio: 7.5 to 1
Fuel system: Solex 31 PICT carburettor, paper element air cleaner, mechanical fuel pump.
Power: 44bhp at 4100rpm
Torque: 64.7 lb ft at 3000rpm
Transmission: Four-speed manual gearbox, syncromesh on all forward gears, ratios — 1st 3.78, 2nd 2.06, 3rd 1.26, 4th 0.93, reverse 3.79. Final drive ratio 4.375. Cable-operated single-plate clutch.
Suspension: Independent front suspension with MacPherson coil spring struts, track control arms and anti-roll bar. Independent rear suspension with double-jointed drive shafts, semi-trailing arms and transverse torsion bars, telescopic shock absorbers.
Steering: Worm and roller, 2.6 turns lock to lock. Negative offset from 8/73, rack and pionion steering from 8/74.
Brakes: Front drums 248mm x 45mm, rear drums 230mm x 40mm. Hydraulic operation with dual circuit.
Wheels and Tyres: Steel disc wheels with four-bolt fixing, 4½J-15, 5.60-15 crossply or 155-15 radial ply tyres.
Length: 4110mm (161.8in)
Width: 1585mm (62.4in)
Height: 1500mm (59in)
Wheelbase: 2420mm
Unladen weight: 890kg (1962lb)
Typical Performance: Maximum speed 78mph, 0-50mph 14.0sec, 0-60mph 20.5sec, 0-70mph 36.0sec, average fuel consumption 26mpg.

Above: 1303S

1303S
*(AUGUST 1972-JULY 1975;
CONVERTIBLE TO JANUARY 1980)*

Engine type: Rear-mounted, horizontally opposed four-cylinder, air-cooled, with two pushrod-operated overhead valves per cylnder. Aluminium alloy cylinder heads (one per pair of cylinders), cast-iron cylinder barrels, magnesium alloy crankcase with four-bearing crankshaft.

Bore: 85.5mm
Stroke: 69mm
Capacity: 1584cc
Compression ratio: 7.5 to 1
Fuel system: Solex 34 PICT carburettor, paper element air cleaner, mechanical fuel pump.
Power: 50bhp at 4000rpm
Torque: 79 lb ft at 2800rpm
Transmission: Four-speed manual gearbox, syncromesh on all forward gears, ratios — 1st 3.78, 2nd 2.06, 3rd 1.26, 4th 0.93, reverse 3.79. Final drive ratio 3.875. Cable-operated single-plate clutch.
Suspension: Independent front suspension with MacPherson coil spring struts, track control arms and anti-roll bar. Independent rear suspension with double-jointed drive shafts, semi-trailing arms and transverse torsion bars, telescopic shock absorbers.
Steering: Worm and roller, 2.6 turns lock to lock. Negative offset from 8/73, rack and pinion steering from 8/74.
Brakes: Front discs, 277mm dia., rear drums 230mm x 40mm. Hydraulic operation with dual circuit.
Wheels and Tyres: Steel disc wheels with four-bolt fixing, 4½J-15, 5.60-15 crossply or 155-15 radial ply tyres (5½J-15 wheels with 175/70-15 tyres optional).
Length: 4110mm (161.8in)
Width: 1585mm (62.4in)
Height: 1500mm (59in)
Wheelbase: 2420mm (95.3in)
Unladen weight: 890kg (1962lb)
Typical Performance: Maximum speed 81mph, 0-50mph 12.2sec, 0-60mph 17.9sec, 0-70mph 30.5sec, average fuel consumption 31mpg.

Special Editions

The following are the best-known limited-edition special Beetles. Most featured special paintwork and upholstery and/or added accessories.

June Beetle (1970).
1500 with orange paintwork, bumper over-riders, wheel trim and heated rear window.

Super Vee Beetle (1971).
1302S with metallic blue or turquoise paintwork, sports steering wheel and Lemmerz road wheels.

World Champion or **Marathon Beetle (1972).**
1300 with 'Marathon Blue' metallic paint and special wheels. Commemorated the Beetle's world record production of 15,007,034.

Black and Yellow Racer (1973).
1303S, yellow wth black bonnet, engine cover and bumpers, slotted front valence, rally seats, 5½-inch wide wheels with 175/70-15 tyres. *Not in UK.*

GT Beetle (1972/3).
1300S (1300 torsion bar chassis with 1600 engine and disc brakes), red, green or yellow paintwork, velour seats, padded facia, tunnel tray, sports wheels. Commemorated UK sales of 300,000.

Jeans Beetle (1974).
1200, yellow with black bumpers, headlamp rims, mirrors and door handles, blue denim seats with back pockets, sports wheels, radio, heated rear window.

Big Beetle (1974).
1303S with blue, green, gold or silver metallic paintwork, velour corduroy seats, luxury carpet, wooden trim on facia and 5½-inch wide wheels with 175/70-15 tyres.

City Beetle (1974).
1303 with red, blue metallic or green metallic paint, special striped upholstery, luxury carpet, radio, heated rear window, sports wheels. *Not in UK.*

Winter Beetle (1974).
1200, 1303 or 1303S with extras including fog-lamps, heavy-duy battery, heated rear window and reversing lights. *Not in UK.*

Sun Beetle (1975).
1300 with sunroof, yellow or orange paintwork, padded facia and sports wheels.

Chocolate Beetle (1975).
1303 with deep brown metallic paintwork, wooden trim on facia and sports wheels.

Last Edition (1978).
200L. The last 600 Beetles to be imported to the UK, 300 of which had silver metallic paintwork and a numbered 'Last Edition' plaque.

Silver Beetle (1981), Mexican).
1200L with silver metallic paintwork and black/white 'tartan' upholstery. Commemorated total Beetle production reaching 20 million. Special '20 million' plaques on engine cover, gear lever and key ring.

Jeans Bug (1982, Mexican).
1200L, red or white paintwork, otherwise similar to 1974 Jeans Beetle.

Special Bug (1982, Mexican).
1200L, red or metallic black paintwork, black instead of chrome trim, special interior features.

Aubergine Beetle (1983, Mexican).
1200L with metallic aubergine paintwork, colour-keyed wheels and interior.

Metallic Ice Blue Beetle (1983, Mexican).
1200L with ice-blue paintwork and colour-keyed interior.

Sunny Bug (1984, Mexican).
1200L with yellow paintwork and colour-keyed interior.

Velvet Red Beetle (1984, Mexican).
1200L with red paintwork, special decor and colour-keyed interior.

Jubilee Beetle (1985, Mexican).
1200L with grey metallic paintwork, green-tinted windows and striped upholstery. Commemorated 50 years of Beetles. Special '50 Jahre Käfer' plaques on side panels and engine cover, sports wheels and Golf GTi steering wheel.

5

Improving the breed

The Volkswagen Beetle was of course conceived as a 'car for the people' and built its reputation on being a no-nonsense, reliable, economical vehicle for everyday transport. It was never intended to be an 'enthusiast's car'. Sportier versions were developed and produced by Porsche, and in the early 1950s the Porsche 356 used many Beetle-derived components including an uprated twin-carburettor version of the original Volkswagen 1131cc engine. Porsche produced a 1086cc 40bhp version for racing in the under-1100cc class; they also enlarged the engine up to 1488cc and 70bhp. The Volkswagen factory always disapproved of any private attempts to modify or tune the Beetle, their view being that anyone who wanted that type of car should buy a Porsche.

But enthusiasts quickly discovered that parts from early Porsches could be fitted to Beetles. The favourite way to improve a Beetle in the 1950s and 1960s was to install a Porsche engine, Porsche brakes and Porsche wheels.

Another option was to fit a supercharger — probably the simplest way of bolting extra power on to an otherwise standard Beetle engine.

Performance conversions which had some degree of VW factory approval, and became very highly regarded as the most reliable way of increasing the Beetle's power, were those produced in Germany by Oettinger. Known as Okrasa conversions, these included twin carburettors, twin-port cylinder heads (made of better material than the stock VW components) and stronger, counter-weighted, long-stroke crank-

shafts (the early VW crankshaft was known to break if subjected to increased power and speed). Okrasa engines were homologated for motorsport for the Beetle and were used quite successfully in international rallies during the 1960s by Scania Vabis, the Swedish Volkswagen importer.

Porsche 356 engines, superchargers and Okrasa engines are now very much collector's items and change hands only rarely and at very high prices.

Numerous other aftermarket conversions for the VW came and went during the 1960s. The Volkswagen factory in Europe stuck rigidly to the standard single-carburettor Beetle engine and neither the Karmann Ghia coupé nor the GT Beetle provided anything extra in the way of performance or handling. However, the VW factories in Brazil and South Africa did produce twin-carb 'high performance' Beetles as limited editions.

For those who want to stick to genuine VW components, there is the possibility of installing an engine from a Type 3 Fastback or Variant, which developed 54bhp in standard 1600cc twin-carburettor form, or the 1.7-litre engine from the Type 4, which produced 68bhp with carburettors and later 80bhp with fuel injection. Both Type 3 and Type 4 engines require extensive re-working of the cooling system for operation in a Beetle as they have crankshaft-mounted fans with ducted inlets. The Type 4 engine has major advantages for performance tuning because the spacing between the cylinders is greater than in the Type 1 or Type 3, which means that there is more scope

Above: Period accessories from the 1950s and 1960s include these cowls for the sloping headlamps, known as 'eyebrows'...

Below: ...and a rear luggage rack. This probably had an adverse effect on the Beetle's handling and rear vision, but supplemented its limited luggage capacity.

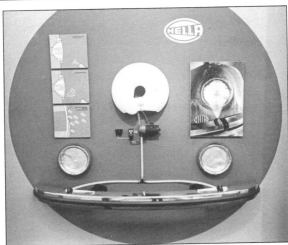

Above: In the early 1970s Hella produced this headlamp wash system for Beetles. The reservoir fitted inside the spare wheel.

Opposite page
Top: 'Okrasa' twin-carb conversions were produced by Oettinger for all Beetle engines, starting with the original 1131cc 25bhp model, and established a lasting reputation as the best-engineered and most reliable way of increasing the Beetle's performance. This is a genuine original Okrasa engine in Keith Seume's 1951 split-window model. Note the magneto.

Bottom: A two-litre Oettinger-engined 1303S, complete with ATS alloy wheels, rally lamps and spoiler, shown on the Volkswagen stand at the 1973 Frankfurt Motor Show.

for modifying the cylinder heads, that there are fewer cooling problems, and that the crankcase is stronger. Type 4 engines, developed to 2.4 litres and 180bhp, were fitted to Beetles by the Austrian Volkswagen importers, Porsche-Salzburg, for motorsport in the mid-1970s and won the European Rallycross Championship. Beetles with Type 4 engines, enlarged to 2.7 litres and 200bhp, now race in the Käfer Cup in Germany.

The continuing popularity of the Beetle in the USA for drag racing, off-road racing and customising has given rise to a vast aftermarket offering performance components. Literally everything is there for the buying, from twin 48IDA Weber carburettors to special custom-made crankcases and from racing gearboxes to turbochargers and nitrous oxide injection. It is possible to build a racing 'VW' engine entirely from aftermarket parts, using no original VW parts whatsoever! However, such undertakings are beyond the scope of the present book, and we shall confine this chapter to 'improving' rather than radically altering the Beetle.

For everyday use, there is still much to be said for keeping the engine standard. In an after-market which focuses primarily on custom shows, and where a 'race' covers only a quarter of a mile and lasts less than 15 seconds, few products are engineered for serious long-term reliability at high speeds. It is a sad fact that

modified Beetles are often seen broken down on the motorway going to or from custom shows, and one wonders what has happened to the Beetle's ability in the 1960s to drive flat-out for the entire length of a motorway or autobahn, when 'maximum speed was cruising speed'.

The Beetle engine's 'unburstable' reputation only applies when power and rpm are restricted by the standard carburettor and inlet system. When this restriction is removed, you can very easily exceed the temperature and stress limits of major components. You can enjoy driving a Beetle even without modifying its engine. Despite the modest power, a 50bhp or even 34bhp

Above: *Oettinger's twin-carb 1600cc Beetle engine developed 70bhp at 4500rpm. Note the retention of a stock exhaust and air filter. Oettinger conversions were favoured uniquely with Volkswagen factory approval.*

Below: *This twin-carb 1600 engine assembled by Autobarn is modelled on the Brazilian VW factory Super Fusca, using Type 3 carburettors. Twin preheat pipes are necessary to prevent icing.*

Beetle can cover the ground surprisingly rapidly and without losing its legendary reliability.

Performance of a 1200 or 1300 Beetle can be enhanced by fitting a larger standard engine — all sizes of engine are interchangeable. The ultimate re-engine-ing is to install the water-cooled flat four from a late-model Type 2, which is 1.9 litres and gives 78bhp. This was the route followed by owners Christine Biggs and Angela Broomfield when they decided to improve their 1972 Marathon Beetle. The conversion, which also included changing the rear suspension from swing-axle to double-jointed, completely renewing the brakes, retrimming the interior and fitting four Recaro seats, took seven years and cost a hard-earned fortune, but the result is probably the best-engineered Beetle yet seen on this planet!

Returning to the simplicity of bolt-on improvements, the most effective is to fit a bigger carburettor, or twin carbs, in place of the Beetle's original single Solex 30, 31 or 34 PICT. Big Boys' Toys, Autocavan, Stateside Tuning, Terry's Beetle Services, Microgiant and others offer a variety of carb conversions for those choosing this option.

A popular carburettor, which fits on the standard Beetle manifold, is the Nikki progressive twin-choke. In this type, one relatively

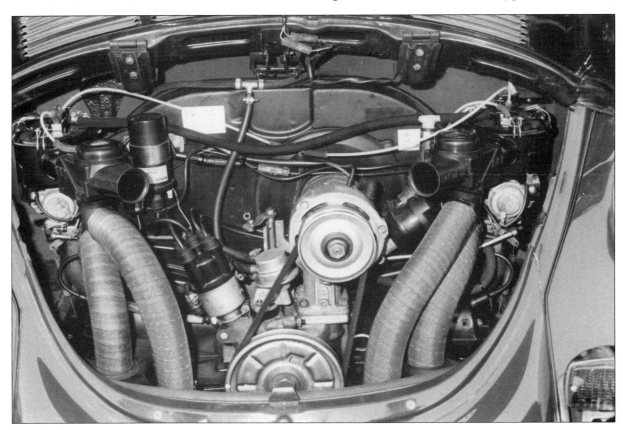

Above: *A single Nikki carburettor installed on the standard manifold is the simplest engine improvement. The gain in performance is small, but there are useful improvements in flexibility and economy.*

small choke operates at low speed and a second choke opens when higher power and higher speeds are required. The gain in power is quite modest, but both driveability and economy are improved.

Next up the performance scale is the Weber 32/36 DFEV, again a progressive twin-choke, but this time necessitating a new manifold. This is designed primarily for the 1600 twin-port engine, and the manifold centre section mates up with the original 1600 end pieces. If fitted with special end pieces, it can also be used on the 1300 or 1500 engines.

Parallel or 'synchronous' twin-choke carburettors are effectively two carburettors in a single body and are normally installed in pairs, giving one choke per cylinder, for racing applications. Weber DCNF and IDA, Solex PII and Dellorto DRLA are carburettors of this type. Other modifications to cylinder heads, valves and camshaft are necessary, of course, when installing these carburettors.

A single twin-choke carb can be fitted to the Beetle engine, placed centrally on a suitable manifold. A Weber 40 DCNF kit is available for 1300 and 1600 twin-port Beetles. The Beetle Cup race cars, with 1641cc, use a single Dellorto 40 DRLA. Power output, with a high-lift camshaft, is about 70bhp.

It is, however, preferable to do away with the T-junction or 'bicycle handlebars' type of inlet manifold required when a single carburettor is installed on a flat four engine, and to fit separate carburettors on each side, mounted directly above the cylinder heads.

Using fairly modest carburettors, such as Weber 32 or 34 ICT or the Kadron-Solex kit made in Brazil for Beetles, a power increase of 25 per-cent can be achieved without any other modifications. This is a straightforward bolt-on conversion — though it should be noted that removing the original manifold, especially the one-piece manifold on single-port engines, is not easy with the engine *in situ.* You have to raise the fan housing, remove the alternator/dynamo support casting, and then solve something of a Chinese puzzle to manoeuvre the manifold away from the engine.

On the early 1200 engines there was adequate space each side for twin carbs, but with the bigger

Above: The most effective suspension improvement is to replace the standard shock absorbers by Bilsteins or Konis.

fan housing and so-called fresh air heating system introduced in 1963, space became very restricted. Access to the sparking plugs, and indeed the carburettors themselves, is a problem. It is advisable to fit long-life plugs such as Bosch platinum which do not need attention for 20,000 or 30,000 miles, and a cooler grade can be fitted for hard driving without risk of fouling in traffic. I would recommend Bosch W7DP for standard or medium-tuned engines.

As well as giving more power, a twin-carb conversion enables the Beetle to rev more freely to 4,500-5,000rpm instead of being restricted to 4,000. This gives a more useful speed range in each gear and is particularly beneficial on hills. Twin carburettors should also eliminate flat spots and icing problems, they can work satisfactorily without a cold-start choke, and fuel consumption should be no worse than with the standard engine. Careful attention should be paid to the throttle linkage which, due to the carburettors being so far apart, can be troublesome if not properly engineered.

Most twin carb kits are available with manifolds for the 1600 twin-port engine. The choice for single-port applications tends to be rather limited; in particular the 1200 engine, which does not have the same cylinder heads as the 1300, is not well catered for. However, Autocavan can supply manifolds to fit twin Weber 32 ICT carbs to the 1200 and this raises the performance of the 1200 to roughly the level of a 1500.

In most cases, with any non-standard carburettors you need to fit an all-centrifugal advance distributor, commonly the Bosch '009', in place of the original vacuum advance type.

There are various aftermarket exhaust systems for the Beetle, but for engines in road-going tune the gains in performance are marginal. The stock Beetle exhaust has a cross-flow configuration with a transverse silencer box. Most aftermarket exhausts have axial-flow silencers which necessitate rather convoluted pipes from the horizontally opposed cylinder heads and terminate in side outlets. There's not really sufficient space for such a system, so part of it usually hangs down below the bodywork, unsightly to the observer and vulnerable to grounding on any uneven road surface.

Changing the camshaft necessitates a complete strip-down of the engine and separation of the crankcase halves. Valve lift can be increased *without* changing the camshaft by fitting offset or 'high ratio' rockers.

If any changes are made which increase the load on the valve train — such as a high-lift camshaft, bigger valves with stronger springs, or high ratio rockers — it is advisable to fit stronger pushrods. The standard alloy pushrods tend to bend and should be replaced by steel rods. The standard rocker shaft assembly can also give trouble at high revs. It is advisable to fit heavy-duty rocker shaft assemblies, such as those made by Scat or Gene Berg, which among features have bolted ends instead of the standard spring clips.

The air-cooled engine has individual cylinder barrels (like liners with fins) and therefore cannot be bored out like a water-cooled cylinder block. However, it can be enlarged very easily by replacing the cylinder barrels and pistons with larger bore items. In most cases, the heads and crankcases will have to be machined to accept the larger bore cylinders. The 1200 and 1300 engines both have 77mm bore cylinders, the difference here being the crankshaft stroke: 64mm for the

1200 and 69mm for the 1300. Larger engines also have the 69mm crank. The 1500 has 83mm cylinders and the 1600mm has 85.5mm cylinders.

Aftermarket pistons and cylinders are available up to 94mm bore which gives 1915cc with the standard crank, while long-stroke crankshafts can further raise the capacity to nearly 2.5 litres.

Such massive increases in capacity, within a crankcase originally designed for 1200cc, will seriously reduce the life of the engine. Large bore cylinders inevitably have shorter cooling fins, so the engine will run much hotter, and there are likely to be other major problems with distortion and oil consumption. For reliable road use, I would not recommend going beyond 1600 or 1700cc, as even at this size the engine will still run significantly hotter than a 1200 or 1300.

If performance *is* radically increased, then a Porsche fan conversion, such as that offered by Stateside Tuning, is recommended. An additional oil-cooler is needed, preferably located outside the engine compartment, together with an uprated oil pump. A sump extension is also essential to increase the volume of oil and overcome the problem of oil surge during fast cornering. It will also provide a little extra cooling, but it will be vulnerable to damage on rough roads. The best solution is to convert to a dry sump system, also available from Stateside Tuning.

Improvements to the Beetle's instrumentation will be covered later in this chapter. However, it should be mentioned here that an oil-temperature gauge is vital. Oil temperature is primarily affected by the car's forward speed. If maximum speed is increased by 10mph, then the oil temperature will rise about 15 deg. C. The safe limit should be regarded as 110 deg. C. This limit is not determined by lubrication criteria — indeed, there are plenty of modern oils that work satisfactorily in other engines at up to 150 deg. C. The important element where the Beetle is concerned is metal temperature: overheating will lead to crankcase distortion, cylinder-head cracking, and burnt valves.

For improved roadholding and handling, the top priorities are a set of heavy duty shock absorbers and a front spoiler. Even when new, the original equipment shock absorbers have insufficient damping for enthusiastic driving. Sports shock absorbers with firmer damping, such as those manufactured by Bilstein or Koni, will do more than anything else to improve the handling and roadholding of a swing-axle Beetle.

Above and below: *Two classic and much sought-after types of steel wheels for Beetles are the Marathon (above) which was fitted to the World Champion special edition Beetle in 1972, and the Rostyle, or Empi Sprint Star (below), available as an accessory in the mid-1970s.*

Right and below: Extra instruments should be at the top of your shopping list of improvements. Instruments can be neatly fitted in panels in place of the grilles on each side of the speedo. Seen in these pictures of Peter Noad's Beetle are instruments from the VDO cockpit range: quartz clock, voltmeter, revcounter, oil temperature and oil pressure gauges.

Below: An alternative instrument arrangement using a centre console. Note also the Moto-Lita steering wheel, parcel shelf and map-reading light. (Christine Biggs)

Above: The ultimate engine conversion for a Beetle is to install the water-cooled flat four (known as 'water-boxer') from the Type 2 Transporter of 1983-1990. This installation was designed and built by Christine Biggs and Andrea Broomfield (with a little help from their friends). With a custom-made exhaust system, the 1.9-litre water-boxer gives 86bhp at the wheels, enabling the Beetle to out-accelerate a Golf GTI. It will do up to 40mpg on unleaded with cleaner exhaust emissions than an air-cooled engine.

Left: Radiator for the water-cooled engine is located in the front of the luggage boot. (Christine Biggs)

Opposite page
A Kamei front spoiler significantly improves the Beetle's stability in cross-winds and its roadholding at high speed.

The main problem with the swing-axle, which is responsible for the oversteer and instability for which Beetles are often criticised, is that wheel camber angle changes as the suspension is deflected. Sudden changes of wheel camber cause loss of road grip. By fitting shock absorbers with firmer damping, the frequency and amplitude of the suspension oscillation are reduced and wheel camber angle is kept more constant.

After fitting Bilstein shock absorbers to my own Beetle, and without making any other changes to the suspension or tyres, I found that on corners where the Beetle previously felt precarious at 50-55mph, it was now quite secure and sure-footed at 65mph. With Bilsteins there is no pitching or swaying on undulating roads at high speed, there is far greater stability on hump-backed bridges and through S-bends, and the Beetle generally feels much more solid and positive.

Bilstein shockers are used by most leading competitors in the World Rally Championship and in off-road racing and touring car racing: they give better performance and last longer than the cheaper alternatives. You may not find them on the shelf at Beetle tuning specialists, and if your main interest is cruising on smooth roads with lowered suspension, then other shockers may be more appropriate. But if you like to think of the Beetle as a rally car and enjoy driving quickly on unclassified roads, then Bilstein shock absorbers are essential. Bilsteins are available for all post-1965 Beetles; the UK distributor is Alan A. Morgan Ltd., whose address will be found among the list of specialists in the next chapter.

Beetles are notorious for being affected by crosswinds, which can make motorway driving an extremely tiring experience. Stability in windy conditions can be improved by fitting a front spoiler, manufactured by Kamei. The spoiler fits under the front bumper and closes the gap between bumper and bodywork. Kamei produced the first front spoiler for a Beetle as long ago as 1953, so can claim to be a world leader in this field, and the design is based on wind tunnel testing. Kamei spoilers are available in the UK from Scotford Ltd.

Roadholding can be further improved by fitting a stiffer front anti-roll bar. Anti-roll bars should never be fitted to the *rear* of a Beetle for road use. The 'Z-bar' which has been standard on the rear of swing-axle Beetles since 1966 must not

Above: Late model slotted engine lids do not have any water baffles and drainage tubes, making the engine vulnerable to damp electrics and corrosion. Aftermarket cowls, produced by Kamei and others, are a popular fitment.

be confused with an anti-roll bar: it has exactly the opposite effect to an anti-roll bar at the rear, and a similar effect to an anti-roll bar at the front, i.e. it reduces oversteer.

The popular notion of modifications to improve roadholding is of lowered suspension and wide wheels. Lowering the rear of a swing-axle car alters the camber angle of the wheels. A degree or two of negative cambering will improve cornering grip, but lowering can increase the risk of damaging the sump or exhaust due to grounding on rough roads. Lowering is accomplished by altering the position of the trailing arm on the splines on the torsion bar. There are different numbers of splines at each end of the bar and, for fine adjustment, it is necessary to rotate the torsion bar relative to its inner anchorage in the opposite direction. One spline in each direction gives an adjustment of just under one degree.

Widening the rear track of a swing-axle Beetle by fitting wider wheels or spacers effectively softens the suspension and lowers the car. (The wheel, being further from the swing-axle pivot exerts more leverage on the torsion bar.) An extra inch on each side (2ins increase in track dimension), preferably with the addition of stiffer shock absorbers, is a simple and effective way of improving handling and roadholding, especially on cars with a Z-bar.

Although wider wheels are advantageous at the rear, at the front they can cause undesirable effects, nameley bump-steer and loss of stability whenever the front wheels are subjected to unequal forces. When considering fitment of wider wheels, you must pay attention to the offset dimension. Offset, which is the distance between the centre line of the rim and the mounting face which bolts to the brake drum or disc brake hub, is marked on the wheel as 'ET' and a figure which is the offset in millimetres.

Generally, offset has to be reduced when rim width is increased, otherwise the wheel (or tyre) will rub on the suspension or brake caliper. If the offset is too small, then steering stability will be poor. A large wheel offset is needed to achieve 'negative steering roll radius' or 'negative steering offset' which provides the self-stabilising steering as pioneered on the Audi 80 and introduced on the 1303 Beetle in 1974.

Beetle wheels up to 1972 were 4-15 with 40mm offset (ET40). Thereafter the standard wheel for torsion bar Beetles was 4½-15 ET34. Optional sports wheels for the 1303S in 1973 were 5½-15 ET26. The 1974 1303 was fitted with 4½-15 ET41 or 5½-15 ET34 and these should not be installed on earlier cars. Karmann Ghia wheels have more offset than Beetle wheels. When buying aftermarket wide wheels, you should check the offset dimension. It is not advisable to go wider than 5½in rims or less than 26mm offset.

The choice of tyre sizes for 15in wheels has widened in recent years and, as alternatives to the standard 155-15, you can fit 175/70-15 on 5in (or wider) rims or 195/65-15 on 5½in rims. These all have the same rolling circumference so maintain the standard gearing and speedo calibration.

The torsion bar front suspension can be lowered, but it is a cut-and-weld job to reposition the central anchorage for the torsion bars within the axle beam. It is often done purely for cosmetic effect, to give the 'Cal-look': there is no advantage in terms of roadholding. Lowering in this way affects the caster angle, making it necessary to fit caster wedges to tilt the beam out at the bottom to compensate. Insufficient caster makes the car unstable at high speed.

The strut front suspension on 1302 and 1303 models can be lowered in the normal way by fitting shorter springs. Lowering the double-jointed rear does not change the camber angle.

Close to the top of your shopping list for improvements should be additional instruments. The Beetle dashboard has only the bare mini-

Above: *Paintwork on the front of the bonnet and wings is highly susceptible to stone chips. Damage can be avoided by fitting a 'bonnet bib' as seen on this GT Beetle. It must be remembered, though, that moisture will accumulate beneath the bib, leading to corrosion, so it should be removed when the car is not being used.*

mum: a speedometer and a fuel gauge. Early models did not even have a fuel gauge.

As stated earlier in this chapter, an oil temperature gauge is essential. With no water to boil, there is no visible warning of steam if the engine overheats. A gauge is therefore the only simple way of monitoring a Beetle engine's operating temperature. The best is manufactured by VDO, using a dipstick sender.

Next in priority is an oil pressure gauge. The VDO pressure gauge comes with a scale range of 0-10 bar or 0-5 bar. The latter is more appropriate for a Beetle, because the normal operating pressure is only about 3 bar (42psi).

These and other matching instruments in the VDO cockpit range, including a revcounter and

voltmeter, are available from leading VW tuning firms, such as Autocavan. Instruments can be fitted in panels replacing the grilles each side of the speedometer, assuming the original radio speaker location is not required. Accessory panels are marketed for various configurations of instruments but, as these are produced in the USA, they are available only for left-hand drive.

As far as bodywork modifications and accessories are concerned, there is a truly vast selection. Beauty is in the eye of the beholder, and if you enjoy chrome-plated dipsticks and neon pink drive shaft boots, there are plenty of people ready to sell you such things. You can give your Beetle the vintage look, with period accessories such as headlamp eyebrows and towel-rail bumpers; the drag race look, with lowered suspension, stinger exhaust and monster tach; or the off-road Baja look with oversize knobbly tyres, cutaway bodywork and spotlamps on the roof. However many Beetles are on the road, you can be sure that there are no two exactly alike!

The imagination of competitors in custom car shows is
truly limitless!

TV·23416

6

Specialists, publications and clubs

There are countless specialists, in Britain and worldwide, who provide parts and services for owners of air-cooled Volkswagens. Many advertise regularly in the VW magazines. The problem is not where to find a Beetle specialist, but which one to choose!

The only way to be sure of maintaining the famous Volkswagen quality and reliability of your Beetle is to fit genuine Volkswagen parts. It may not be generally known that genuine parts for Beetles can still be obtained from official Volkswagen Audi dealers. Routine parts, such as fan belts, exhaust gaskets and throttle cables are normally available off-the-shelf, while the slower moving items can be obtained within a few days.

Outside of the franchised V.A.G. dealer network, there are a few independent specialists who supply genuine VW factory parts — notably Autobarn in Pershore and Karmann Classics in Hove — and whose catalogues cover a range of parts from small items of trim to complete floorpans.

It is very important to be aware of the distinction between these genuine Volkswagen parts and the so-called aftermarket or 'pattern' parts that are widely available for Beetles. In fact there is a massive worldwide industry producing Beetle replacement parts which might be made anywhere from England or Italy to Brazil or Taiwan. Even when parts are advertised as being manufactured in countries where there are

known to be VW factories, such as Germany or Brazil, it must not be presumed that the parts have been made by Volkswagen or that they are of Volkswagen quality.

Some replacement parts are very cheap and many are of poor quality. There have been plenty of cases of chrome tailpipes and bumpers that go rusty in a few months, floorpans with shoddy and flimsy mountings for the seats, and heat exchangers that are ineffective due to lack of sufficient fins.

If your need is simply to keep the car on the road at minimum cost and you do not cover a high mileage or drive quickly, then aftermarket replacements *may* be satisfactory. However, if you have chosen to own a Beetle because of its superior build quality, reliability and longevity, then you will not wish to degrade these qualities by fitting parts manufactured elsewhere to lower standards.

There are similarly varying standards with regard to tuning parts. Some so-called tuning parts are only intended for show! Parts designed for quarter-mile drag racing are probably not proven over high mileages and will not have the durability needed for rallying or even long-distance motorway driving.

Before purchasing any tuning parts or services, it is essential to discuss your intended application with the vendor and be aware that many 'highly tuned' Beetles are used only for low-speed cruising or static displays! If you are going to drive your Beetle hard and fast, you should go only to firms which have a good track record in motorsport.

It is not possible to list all the Beetle specialists here: the following is a selection of the better-known. Please note that inclusion in these lists should not be taken as a guarantee of any company's standards of quality or service, nor is omission intended to imply that a company cannot be recommended.

Tuning, Motorsport Preparation, Customising and Restoration

Arnie Levics, Leigh Road Garage, Street, Somerset BA16 0HA. Tel. 0458 42707. *Engineering services and parts.*

Autobarn, Manor Farm House, Kersoe, Pershore, Worcestershire WR10 3JD. Tel. 0386 710780. *Genuine Volkswagen factory parts including new bodyshells, chassis and engines. Specialists in Mexican and Brazilian Beetles.*

Autocavan, 103 Lower Weybourne Lane, Badshot Lea, Farnham, Surrey GU9 9LG. Tel. 0252 333891. *More than 50 agents and branches nationwide. Very wide range of tuning parts and accessories and engineering services. Successfully involved in all types of motorsport since 1968.*

The Beetle People, 2 Burnett Road, Erith, Dartford, Kent. Tel. 0322 347513. *Restoration, secondhand parts.*

Beetle Specialist Workshop, Ballards Place, Lardiston, Tenbury Wells, Worcestershire WR15 8JR. Tel. 058 470348. *Restoration and motorsport preparation, specialists in trials and off-road cars.*

Bernard Newbury, 1 Station Road, Leigh-on-Sea, Essex SS9 1ST. Tel. 0702 710211. *Coachwork and interior trimming, carpets, headlining, repairs to convertible tops and sunroofs.*

Big Boy's Toys, Unit 1, Motherwell Way, West Thurrock, Essex RM16 1NR. Tel. 0708 861827. *Tuning parts, accessories, customising, performance engines for Beetle Cup racing.*

Francis Tuthill's Workshop, Wardington, near Banbury, Oxfordshire OX17 1RY. Tel. 0295 750514. *Engineering services, race and rally preparation and restoration. Many years' experience rallying Beetles. Cars for sale.*

German Car Company, Britavia House, Southend Airport, Southend-on-Sea, Essex SS2 6YU. Tel. 0702 530440. *Customising, tuning and restoration parts.*

Haselock, 22 Slingsby Close, Attleborough Fields, Nuneaton, Warwickshire CV11 6RP. Tel 0203 328343. *Restoration specialists.*

John Forbes Automotive, 7 Meadow Lane, Edinburgh EH8 9NR. Tel. 031 667 9767. *Specialised service, parts and restoration.D*

Karmann Classics, 96 Northease Drive, Hove, Sussex BN3 8LH. Tel. 0273 424330. *Genuine Volkswagen factory parts.*

Karmann Connection, 4 High Street, Hadleigh, Essex SS7 2PB. Tel. 0702 551766. *Restoration parts.*

Left: Francis Tuthill's Workshop at Banbury carries out exceptionally thorough and properly-engineered body-off restorations. Tuthill also specialises in motorsport preparation — he has a great deal of experience rallying Beetles, having driven them on events such as the RAC

Kingfisher Kustoms, Unit 22, Mornington Road, Smethwick, Warley, West Midlands B66 2JE. Tel. 021 558 9135. *Off-road racing specialists, Buggies and Baja conversions, tuning parts.*

Limited Edition, Warrington Road, High Legh, near Knutsford, Cheshire WA16 0RT. Tel. 0925 757575. *Tuning, customising and restoration parts.*

John Maher Racing, Unit 16, Albany Trading Estate, Albany Road, Chorlton, Manchester M21 1AZ. Tel. 061 8815225. *Engineering services, tuning, racing preparation.*

Microgiant, Unit 7, Westfield Close, Rawreth Industrial Estate, Rawreth Lane, Rayleigh, Essex SS6 9RL. *Engineering services, tuning, racing preparation.*

Alan A. Morgan Ltd., Europa House, Lichfield Road, Brownhills, W. Midlands WS8 6JP. Tel. 0543 37511. *Distributor for Bilstein shock absorbers.*

Scotford Ltd., Marriage Hill, Bidford-on-Avon, Warwickshire B50 4EP. Tel. 0789 772409. *Kamei spoilers.*

Southern Carburetters, Unit 6, Nelson Trading Estate, Morden Road, Wimbledon, London SW19 3BL. Tel. 081 540 8128. *Weber and Solex carburettors.*

Stateside Tuning, Unit 3, Enterprise Works, Alexandra Road, Enfield, Middlesex EN3 7EH. Tel. 081 805 4865. *Engineering services, tuning, motorsport preparation. Many years' experience rallying Beetles. Wide range of performance parts.*

Terry's Beetle Services, Shirley Garage, Shirley Gardens, Hanwell, London W7 3PT. Tel. 081 567 3165. *Tuning, customising, restoration. Drag racing specialists.*

Volks Bits, 800 Pershore Road, Selly Park, Birmingham B29 7NG. Tel. 021 472 4285. *Tuning, customising and standard parts.*

VUU Tools, 338 Bradford Road, Liversedge, West Yorkshire WF15 6BY. Tel. 0924 402860. *Specialist VW tools for DIY. Mail order only.*

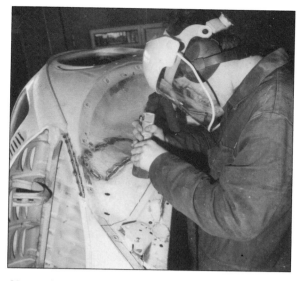

Above: *A section of the bodyshell which has previously been bodged with small patches will be cut away completely and replaced with a new panel at Tuthill's Workshop.*

Below: *Autocavan, based in Farnham but with more than 50 branches and agents nationwide, keeps a comprehensive stock of replacement parts for Beetles. Pictured here are front and rear wings for various models.*

VW Books, 25 Cambridge Road, Cosby, Leicester LE9 5SH. Tel. 0533 866686. *Workshop manuals and all other Volkswagen books. Mail order only.*

VW Dream Machine, URO Automotive, Unit 21, Fort Industrial Park, Dunlop Way, Birmingham B35 7AR. Tel. 021 7494700. *Nationwide network of agents. Customising, tuning and restoration parts.*

Wizard Roadsters, 373 Buckingham Avenue, Slough SL1 4LU. Tel. 0753 551555. *Fibreglass body parts, Roadster, Convertible and Baja conversions, customising.*

Above: Front axle beams for torsion bar Beetles are readily available, including adjustable types for lowered suspension.

Replacement Parts

Ace Auto Spares, 125 Greengate Street, Plaistow, London E13 0BG. Tel. 081 470 9782.

Autocavan, 103 Lower Weybourne Lane, Badshot Lea, Farnham, Surrey GU9 9LG. Tel. 1252 333891. *More than 50 agents and branches nationwide.*

Euro Car Parts, Midland Terrace, Victoria Road, Park Royal, London NW10 6DR. Tel. 081 963 0555.

German and Swedish, Space Ways, North Feltham Trading Estate, Feltham, Middlesex TW14 0TH. Tel. 081 893 1688. *More than 25 agents and branches nationwide.*

URO Automotive, Unit 21, Fort Industrial Park, Dunlop Way, Birmingham B35 7AR. Tel. 021 7494700. *More than 100 agents nationwide.*

Volkspares, 104 Newlands Park, Sydenham, London SE26 5NA. Tel. 081 778 7766. *More than 20 agents and branches nationwide.*

Volkswares, 173 Loughborough Road, Leicester LE4 5LR. Tel. 0533 669998.

Insurance

Bain Clarkson Ltd., P.O. Box 27, Falcon House, The Minories, Dudley, West Midlands, DY2 8PF. Tel. 0384 455011. *Offer various classic car insurance schemes for club members including agreed value and limited mileage cover*

Herts Insurance Consultants, Portland House, 29 Basbow Lane, Bishops Stortford, Herts, CM23 2NA. Tel. 0279 506090. *Specialise in insurance of all VWs including modified and customised. Insurers of Christine Biggs' modified water-cooled Beetle. Agreed value and limited mileage cover available.*

Hoddesdon Insurance Consultants, 46 Ware Road, Hoddesdon, Herts, EN11 9NU. Tel. 0992 470698. *Specialist insurance for club members including modified, customised or high-performance vehicles and agreed value cover.*

Rushton's, 190 St Albans Road, Watford, Herts, WD2 4AT. Tel. 0923 237111. *Specialise in classic car and agreed value insurance.*

Magazines

The three major Volkswagen magazines published in the UK are all independent of the Volkswagen factory and Volkswagen importers. Published monthly, they are on sale through newsagents as well as by mail order subscription.

VW Motoring, Published by Warners Group, The Maltings, West Street, Bourne, Lincolnshire PE10 9PH. Tel. 0778 393652. *First published in 1961 as Safer Motoring. Covers all aspects of VW and Audi models, air-cooled and water-cooled.*

VolksWorld, Published by Link House Magazines Ltd., Dingwall Avenue, Croydon CR9 2TA. Tel. 081 686 2599. *First published in 1987. Exclusively air-cooled, specialising in customising and drag racing.*

Volkswagen Audi Car, Published by Autometrix Publications, Market Chambers, High Street, Toddington, Bedfordshire LU5 6BY. Tel. 0525 874019. *First published in 1982. Concentrates mostly on water-cooled models, especially Golf GTi and Audi quattro, but sometimes features Beetles.*

Beetle Jargon

Auto-stick. Semi-automatic transmission.

Billet. Applies to accessories or components machined from the solid, instead of being cast or moulded.

Bra. Vinyl cover for lower part of bonnet and front wings to protect bodywork from stone damage.

BRM wheels. Mid-1960s alloy wheels for Beetles, sold by Speedwell.

Bud vase. A vase for flower buds which fitted on the facia. (This was an official Volkswagen accessory in the 1950s.)

Bug. American name for Beetle.

Cabrio. Abbreviation of Cabriolet, the 'posh' name for a Beetle Convertible.

Cal-look. The original and longest-surviving customising fashion which started in Southern California in the 1960s, derived from the style of drag racing Beetles of that era. Principal elements of the Cal-look are lowered suspension, alloy wheels and removal of unnecessary trim.

Deck lid. American term for engine cover. More applicable to large US limousines which have a large flat luggage boot at the rear, resembling a 'deck'.

Dog house. The revised oil cooler introduced for the twin-port engines in 1970 with an extension, or 'dog house', on the front of the fan housing.

Double-jointed. Applies to Beetles with semi-trailing arm rear suspension with two universal joints in each drive shaft (as distinct from the swing-axle suspension which has only one joint in each shaft).

Dub. Abbreviation of 'Vee-Dub'.

Elephant's feet. The very large circular type of tail-lamps introduced in 1972.

Europa bars. The broader, sturdier bumpers introduced in 1967.

Eyebrows. Cowls which fitted over the top of the sloping headlamps, popular as accessories in the early 1960s.

Looker. Abbreviation of 'Cal-looker'.

Marathon wheels. Special steel wheels (made by Lemmerz) which were a feature of the World Champion or Marathon Beetle in 1972.

NOS. Abbreviation of 'new old stock' which refers to unused but obsolete parts (i.e. new parts for old models which have been lying in a warehouse for many years). NOS is also an abbreviation of 'nitrous oxide system', a means of boosting the power of engines in drag racing.

Other magazines for the Beetle enthusiast obtainable in the UK are: **Bugpower** (on subscription from Aircool Publications, 22 Campion House, Bracknell, Berkshire RG12 1PG) which contains tuning, DIY and technical information; **Hot VWs and Dune Buggies** (published in the USA by Wright Publishing Co Inc, PO Box 2260, Costa Mesa, California 92628) which features customising, drag racing, off-road racing and DIY technical information; and **The International Vintage Volkswagen Magazine** which caters for 'serious collectors' and specialises in vintage VWs, military VWs, special-bodied VWs and other rarities, available on subscription from IVVM, 194 Old Church Rd., St Leonards-on-Sea, East Sussex TN38 9HD.

Some clubs, notably the **Volkswagen Owners Club Great Britain**, the **Mexican Brazilian Beetle Register** and the **Historic Volkswagen Club**, produce regular newsletters/magazines which contain useful information on DIY and parts availability.

The classic car magazines, such as **Popular Classics** and **Practical Classics**, also contain useful information on restoration services, DIY, parts for old cars, insurance, clubs and events.

Beetle Jargon

Oval. Refers to Beetles with the oval-shaped rear window (1953-1957).

009. All-centrifugal advance Bosch distributor used on most modified Beetle engines in place of the normal vacuum advance type. '009' comes from the last three digits of the part number.

Pope's nose. The number plate lamp on split-window Beetles (1943-early 1953).

Pop-outs. Hinged opening rear side windows (a factory fitted option but rarely seen in the UK).

Resto-Cal. Combination of the Cal-look with the style of an earlier restored model.

Semaphores. The early type of turn signals.

Single port. Refers to cylinder heads with a single inlet port for each pair of cylinders, as used on 1200, 1500 and pre-1971 1300 engines.

Split. Refers to Beetles with the divided rear window (pre-1953).

Stick-shift. Semi-automatic transmission.

Stinger. Megaphone exhaust used in drag racing.

Suicide doors. Rear-hinged, front-opening doors, as fitted to the 1936-37 prototype Beetles and now sometimes incorporated as a customising feature.

Thing. American name for the VW 181 multi-purpose vehicle.

Tin. Term used for the sheet metal cooling ducting surrounding the engine.

Towel rail. Bumpers fitted to pre-1967 American-spec Beetles with an extra 'rail' above the main bumper.

Trekker. British name for the VW 181 multi-purpose vehicle.

Twin port. Refers to cylnder heads with a separate port for each cylinder, i.e. two per pair, as used on 1600 and 1300 engines from 1971.

Vee-Dub. Abbreviation of 'vee-double-you'.

Vent wings. Opening quarter lights.

Vert. Abbreviation of convertible.

W lid. The engine cover fitted to split-window Beetles. (The profile of indentations and ridges in the pressing resembles the letter W.)

Z-bar. A supplementary torsion bar fitted to the rear suspension of swing-axle Beetles (from 1966) which has the opposite effect to an anti-roll bar.

Books

Unsurprisingly, a huge number of books have been written about the Volkswagen Beetle. The following is a selection of some of the more noteworthy titles, which are relevant to this publication. Some may now be out of print, but can still be found (and are worth seeking) in second-hand shops or at auto-jumbles. Those that are currently in print can be purchased from specialist motoring bookshops; a few may be found in general bookshops.

The Beetle: The Chronicles of the People's Car. By Hans-Rudiger Etzold. In three volumes: Vol. 1 Production and Evolution Facts and Figures 1945-1985; Vol. 2 Design and Evolution — The Story; Vol. 3 Beetlemania. Haynes Publishing Group, 1988.

How To Keep Your Volkswagen Alive: A Manual Of Step-By-Step Procedures For The Compleat Idiot. By John Muir. Robert Bentley Inc, USA 1969 (revised 1988). *Covers all air-cooled models up to 1985.*

Illustrated Volkswagen Buyer's Guide. Peter Vack. Motorbooks International, USA 1993. *An overview of all Volkswagens from Beetle to Passat and Corrado.*

Left: *Autobarn, near Pershore, can supply genuine VW factory parts such as these floorpans, which are superior to some of the aftermarket items available elsewhere.*

Below: *Comparison of a genuine VW factory heat exchanger with a cheaper aftermarket example. Reduced fins on the latter result in inferior heating.*

Practical Classics On VW Beetle Restoration.
Brooklands Books. *Reprinted articles from the monthly* Practical Classics *magazine.*

Volkswagen Beetle Step-By-Step Service Guide. Lindsay Porter & Dave Pollard. Porter Publishing, 1994. *Illustrated instructions for servicing and maintenance.*

Volkswagen Bug! The People's Car.
By Ray Miller. The Evergreen Press, USA, 1984. *A detailed photographic record of production changes, year by year.*

Volkswagen Of America Official Service Manuals. Robert Bentley Inc, USA. *Two volumes covering Type 1 1966-1969 and Type 1 1970-1979.*

The VW Beetle: A Collector's Guide.
Jonathan Wood. Motor Racing Publications, 1983. *An accurate development history, including the Karmann Ghia models.*

The 1949-1959 VW Beetle. Bob Wilson. Beeman Jorgensen Inc, USA, 1994. *A comprehensive guide to authenticity in Beetles of the period.*

VW Beetle and Transporter: Guide To Purchase and DIY Restoration.
By Lindsay Porter. Haynes Publishing Group, 1986. *A fully illustrated step-by-step manual for all restoration tasks, with guidelines for buyers.*

VW Beetle Coachbuilts and Cabriolets 1940-1960. By Bob Shaill and Keith Seume. Bay View Books, 1993. *Covers both well-known and rare special-bodied Beetles.*

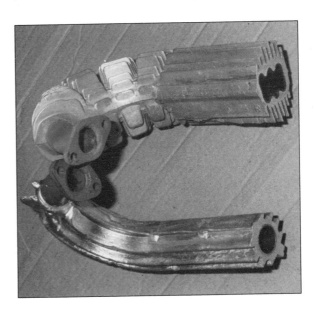

VW Beetle Custom Handbook. Keith Seume. Bay View Books, revised 1993. *Practical guidance on customising and performance tuning.*

VW Beetle Gold Portfolio 1935-1967 *and* **VW Beetle Gold Portfolio 1968-1991.** Compiled by R.M. Clarke. Brooklands Books, 1993. *Useful compilations of road tests and other Beetle articles from different motoring magazines.*

VW Beetle in Motorsport. By Peter Noad. Windrow & Greene Automotive, 1993. *The illustrated history of Beetle sporting activities, from hillclimbs and trials to drag racing, rallying and circuit racing.*

VW Beetle: Restoration, Preparation, Maintenance. Jim Tyler. Osprey Publishing, 1994. *A guide to servicing, restoring, maintaining and modifying the Beetle.*

Above: *Stateside Tuning, in Enfield, Middlesex, offers a wide range of engine tuning and modifications, including fitting a Porsche 911 cooling fan.*

Clubs

There are more than 100 Volkswagen clubs in the UK alone. Many are just small local groups who meet regularly at a pub or at VW events; some are national clubs or registers catering for a specific model (such as the Marathon Beetle Register and the Trekker Club of GB); some cater for both air-cooled and water-cooled VWs, although many are exclusively air-cooled; and a few (less than a handful) are registered with the RAC Motor Sports Association for participation in motor sport events. Comprehensive lists of clubs are published in *VW Motoring* and *Volksworld* magazines. In many cases, the attitude of the members can be gauged by the name of the club. You can expect the 'Yo-Yo V-Dubbers', the 'No H2O Vee Dub Club', the 'Buggist Monks' and 'Captain Chaos and his Air-Cooled Crew' to have plenty of attitude!

The following is a selection of the better-known and more 'responsible' clubs for Beetle owners in the UK. (Note that club secretaries change and there can be no guarantee that the contact address is, or will remain, correct.)

Volkswagen Owners Club Great Britain,
PO Box 7, Burntwood, Walsall, Staffs WS7 8SB. *The National club, established in 1953. Regular 50-page magazine, mutual aid scheme (to help members who break down). affiliated to the RAC and the Classic Trials Association (for motorsport), organiser of the British Volkswagen festival at Malvern, The Clee Hills Classic Trial and the VW Audi National Autotests. The VWOC (GB) has subsidiary regional clubs in Bedfordshire, Derbyshire, Lancashire, Lincolnshire, Oxfordshire, Shropshire, Staffordshire, Wiltshire and Worcestershire, plus a Trials Car Register and a Semi-Automatic Register, and has contacts with VW clubs in other countries.*

Mexican-Brazilian Beetle Register,
11 Foldgate View, Ludlow, Shropshire SY8 1NB. *Caters especially to owners of Beetles manufactured in Mexico and Brazil (this includes current developments and brand-new cars). Information on personal imports, conversions to UK spec. and lhd to rhd, availability of new genuine VW factory parts. Regular 16-page newsletter.*

Historic Volkswagen Club, 28 Longnor Road, Brooklands, Telford, Salop TF1 3NY. *Originally specialised in split-window and oval-window Beetles, now caters for all 6-volt models. Information on parts for these early models. Regular 12-16 page newsletter. Organiser of the Classic VW Festival at Bromsgrove.*

Volkswagen Cabriolet Owners Club GB, 12 Overlea Avenue, Deganwy, Gwynedd LL31 9TH. *For owners of Karmann-built Cabrios. Information on hoods and headlinings, insurance values. Organiser of International Cabriolet Owners Festival. Quarterly magazine.*

Leicestershire & Warwickshire VW Owners Club, 36 Marston Road, Leicester LE4 7FE. *Organiser of the annual Stanford Hall VW Festival.*

London & Thames Valley VW Owners Club, 66 Pinewood Green, Iver Heath, Buckinghamshire SL0 0HQ. *Monthly magazine, insurance services, overseas trips. Organiser of the annual Stonor Park VW Festival.*

Lothians Volkswagen Club, 11/3 Ferry Road Drive, Edinburgh. *Organiser of the annual Scottish VW Owners Festival at Doune*

Hampshire Volkswagen Owners Club, 105 Monarch Way, West End, Southampton SO3 3JR.

Kent Volkswagen Enthusiasts Club, 58 Rochester Street, Chatham, Kent ME4 6RR.

Marathon Beetle Register, 20 Staniwell Rise, Scunthorpe, S. Humberside DN17 1TF. *For 1972 'World Champion' special edition Beetles.*

Semi-Auto Beetle Register, Glenside, Treliever Road, Mabe Burnthouse, Cornwall TR10 9EX. *Information on parts, specialists and repair procedures for the Automatic Stick-Shift and Saxomat Beetles.*

VW Drag Racing Club, 51 Leigh Road, Wimborne, Dorset. *Organiser of the British VW Drag Racing Championships.*

Above: *From road test collections to histories to manuals, there are plenty of books about Beetles...*

Below: *...and plenty of magazines, too. Safer Motoring, the original title of the magazine now known as VW Motoring, was first published in 1961. Beetling evolved from the club magazine of the VWOC; after 292 monthly issues, it ceased publication in this format in 1982 when the publisher launched Volkswagen Audi Car.*

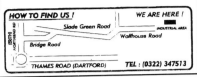

7

Living with a Beetle

Beetles have a unique charisma and attract a great deal of attention, despite the fact that they have been produced in greater numbers (21 million and still counting) and sold in more countries of the world than any other car. If you have a nice-looking example, you can expect passers-by, young and old, to stop and admire it and often to chat to you about Beetles. Everyone recognises a Beetle and most people know a little about them, though few are actually aware that Beetles are still being produced in Mexico.

Drivers of Beetles will often wave or flash their lights to one another as they pass, so be ready to respond! This was a popular practice in the 50s and 60s when VWs were quite rare in Britain and owners regarded themselves as members of an exclusive club. As Beetles became more common-place the wave disappeared but the scenario has now turned full circle: Beetle drivers again see themselves as different from 'ordinary' motorists (a popular sticker proclaims 'It's not a car, it's a Volkswagen') and the wave has returned.

Servicing and Maintenance

The Beetle does not have any antifreeze, hoses or water-pump, but it needs more service and maintenance than a modern water-cooled car. It is very important to change the oil frequently — preferably every 2,000 miles — and to check the valve clearances at the same interval.

The oil should be monograde SAE 30HD (such as Castrol CRI 30, available from VW specialists). There is no oil filter, only a crude strainer which should be cleaned at each oil change. Later Beetles do not have a sump drain plug, so you are obliged to remove the strainer to drain the oil, which makes the operation annoyingly messy! The oil level should be checked regularly as the sump capacity is small — only two-and-a-half litres — and if the level is low there is a risk of oil starvation due to surge when cornering.

Although access to the valves and rockers is from underneath the car, adjustment is quite easy. There have been changes in the specified valve clearance over the years, but for most engines the recommended figure is now 0.15mm (.006in) for inlet and exhaust. Number 3 exhaust valve is the most susceptible to overheating and the clearance of this valve should err on the generous side. Condition and correct fitment of the rocker box gaskets are important; as these are towards the bottom of the engine, any leaks can cause serious oil loss.

Also vital is the condition of the fanbelt. If it fails, the engine will overheat very rapidly. A spare fanbelt should always be carried in the car, together with a 21mm socket or spanner to fit the nut on the generator pulley (conveniently the same size as a sparking plug spanner). A spare fanbelt was also supplied with new Beetles from the factory. The generator pulley is in two parts, enabling belt tension to be adjusted by inserting or removing shims between the two halves of the pulley. Spare shims are kept between the outer half of the pulley and the nut. Correct tension has been achieved when the belt can be deflected about half an inch by thumb pressure.

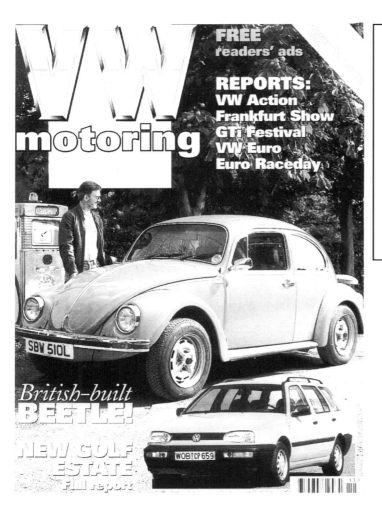

Pre-1972 engines had an oil bath air cleaner which needs servicing every 3,000 miles, and the torsion bar front suspension requires regular application of a grease gun. The ball-joint type has four greasing points which, according to the latest service schedule, need attention every 20,000 miles. The pre-1965 link-pin type had eight greasing points, needing lubrication every 1,500 miles.

The rear brakes do more work than they would on a front-wheel-drive car and should be inspected every 3,000 miles. There are holes in the back plates (which should be covered with rubber plugs) enabling the thickness of the linings to be checked visually. To remove the drum from the drive shaft you have to undo a 36mm castellated nut which is very tight. It is torqued to 250 lb ft, necessitating a heavy-duty socket, 3/4-inch torque drive wrench and strong muscles! The car itself will need to be securely anchored.

Most other aspects of Beetle maintenance are fairly normal, although replacing the clutch cable, should it be necessary, is a pain, especially on rhd cars. Replacing the exhaust is easier than on a front-engined car because it is more compact and the pipe joints have V-section asbestos-type sealing rings and do not rely on a tight metal-to-metal seal.

Driving Technique

The Beetle has been widely criticised for its lack of performance and poor roadholding, but these criticisms have not, in general, been made by any of the millions of people who have owned and regularly driven Beetles. Nor have the alleged shortcomings prevented Beetles from being very successful in motorsport!

In absolute terms, the standard Beetle is a slow car: its 0-60mph acceleration time is about twice the present-day average and its maximum speed is some 20 or 30mph below what can be achieved by nearly every modern saloon. The Beetle's performance has hardly changed since the days when contemporary saloons were the Ford Prefect, Austin Devon and Standard Ten.

There are times, particularly on hills, when the Beetle feels pathetically slow. But in other situations, it can actually be quite quick. The Beetle has a short movement on the accelerator pedal, a limited rev range (maximum is not much over 4,000rpm), and quite low gearing with little more than 20mph available in first, 40mph in second and 60mph in third. Consequently a Beetle driver

Above: *Engine oil needs to be changed frequently — preferably every 2,000 miles. On later models there is no drain plug and the strainer plate has to be loosened to drain the oil. The strainer should, in any case, be removed and cleaned as there is no other filter.*

Below: *Valve clearances should be checked frequently as any loss of clearance will rapidly lead to a burnt valve. Access, from beneath the engine, is not difficult.*

Below: *The third crucial servicing item is fanbelt tension. Adjustment is by means of shims between the two halves of the pulley. A spare fanbelt should be carried in the car.*

Above: There are numerous festivals and shows for Beetle enthusiasts. This is part of the concours d'elegance display at the Stanford Hall festival organised by the Leicestershire and Warwickshire VW Owners Club each year at the beginning of May.

Below: Cathy Pike and Chris Dalton's 1963 'California Dream' at the Volksworld National Show in 1994. Besides the picnic (!), the car is fitted with numerous genuine EMPI accessories from the 1960s. Cathy and Chris have won 'Best of Show' awards with this Beetle.

tends to be driving 'flat-out' all the time, whereas drivers of other cars rarely use more than half throttle and half maximum revs.

By using the accelerator like an on-off switch and using every last rpm in every gear, which is the traditional technique for driving a Beetle, even a 34bhp 1200 can make fairly rapid progress and more than keep up with other traffic in town and on secondary roads. Experienced Beetle drivers adopt an anticipatory technique, so that they are already accelerating when an overtaking opportunity presents itself!

When cornering, Beetles tend to oversteer, which means that the rear will skid first and, if you lose control, the car will spin — in contrast to other cars which tend to run wide. If you try to go round a corner too fast in an understeering car, you will go off the road forwards into a ditch; in an oversteering Beetle, you will go into the ditch backwards.

Although the ultimate cornering speed of a Beetle will obviously never be as high as that of a Golf GTi or Audi quattro, given good tyres and effective shock absorbers (see Chapter 5) a Beetle will corner perfectly safely at speeds as high as any normally enthusiastic driver would use, at least on dry roads. In the wet, a little more caution is advisable. As in all cars, but more so in a Beetle, you should try to avoid having to brake in the

---

Extracts from the Volkswagen Driver's Instruction Manual, 1957.

With the Standard Model, shifting to a lower gear is done as follows:

1 Release accelerator pedal and depress clutch pedal.
2 Place gearshift lever in neutral position.
3 Release clutch pedal and depress accelerator pedal at the same time, the amount of this intermediate feeding of gas depends on the speed of the car.
4 Depress clutch pedal and shift to lower gear.
5 Release clutch pedal steadily and at the same time step on accelerator pedal. After a short period of practice, you will take pleasure in the correct handling and the shifting of gears and obtain the utmost satisfaction from the efficient performance of your new Volkswagen.

Try out your brakes at intervals so that you know how they will react in case of emergency, but make sure there is no vehicle immediately behind you when doing so.

The direction indicators lie outside the driver's view. However the red light with two arrows will serve as a reminder in case you have forgotten to turn the indicator off. The direction indicator switch can be reached without taking the hand off the steering wheel.

Wash your new car frequently during the first weeks. This practice will be of great advantage to the finish. For washing your car you need a soft sponge for the body, a soft brush for the wheels, a sturdy long-handled brush for the chassis, and plenty of clear water. For drying the car you need a chamois.

Insects are caught especially during the night, in hot weather, by fenders, headlights and front hood, Once baked on they can hardly be removed with water and sponge but should be treated with lukewarm soap-solution.

The tank has a capacity of 40 litres, sufficient for a drive of over 500 kilometres. Under normal conditions, the fuel tap should be set at position 'I' while the car is in operation. If the engine begins to stutter as a result of lack of fuel, just turn the tap to '2'. A fuel reserve of 5 litres will then last for a further drive of about 60 kilometres. It is important to reset the tap at position 'I' when refilling the tank, otherwise there will be danger of running out of fuel on the road.

Do not forget the shut the fuel tap when parking on a grade with the rear end of the car downwards.

The door hinges should be oiled at every lubrication service or, better, once a week after dust and dirt have been removed. Door cylinder locks should be treated with graphite only. Blow a small quantity of powdered graphite through the key hole.

Your Volkswagen is a car that 'hugs' the road in an excellent way, and does not roll when taking a turn. Your car has an extraordinary capacity for acceleration. Yet the feeling of security and safety which you will acquire after a few miles should not tempt you to become careless. Be particularly careful when driving on wet or icy roads for even a Volkswagen is apt to skid when not driven carefully under such conditions.

---

middle of a corner. The Beetle is more secure if you can maintain a constant power throughout the corner, without either harsh acceleration or braking.

While you should never experience or practise a tail slide on the public road, it is a good idea to get the feel of oversteer, and the opposite lock needed to control it, either through tuition at a skid-pan school or by taking part in autotests on grass, organised by a car club.

Motorsport

Beetles can take part in all types of motorsport, ranging from the street class of drag racing where you can drive your bog-standard 34bhp 1200 for a quarter-mile in a straight line against the clock, up to international rallycross where you need four-wheel drive, 500 horsepower, a full safety roll-cage and fireproof clothing, plus superstrong muscles and lightning-quick reactions to drive over a cross between a ploughed field and a tank-testing course at 100mph with the windscreen plastered with mud.

Drag racing is cheap and simple at the street class level. All you need to do is get away smartly from the lights and change up through the gears at peak revs. It is run on a handicap basis, so you do not need a powerful car to win. Details can be obtained from the VW Drag Racing Club, whose address is given in Chapter 6.

Classic trials and autotests are the next cheapest events. You do not need a high-powered car, but you do need a level of skill and driving technique which can only be learnt by experience. Classic trials involve driving up steep muddy hills — something at which Beetles have always excelled. Autotests call for complicated 'parking' manoeuvres and slaloms against the clock. The Volkswagen Owners Club of Great Britain organises events of this type and is also invited to events organised by other clubs around the country.

Circuit racing for Beetles began in Britain in 1992. Known as the Beetle Cup, it is promoted by Big Boys' Toys and consists of a series of races at Brands Hatch, Oulton Park, Donington and other major circuits. Already it has proved immensely popular, both with competitors and spectators. The Beetle Cup is undoubtedly one of the cheapest forms of motor racing, though you would still have to budget for at least £5,000 for a season's

Above and below: Until its closure in 1993 the biggest VW festival was VW Action, held every September. It included camping, trade displays, driving competitions, concours d'elegance, and arena events such as the 'Bug Push'. Shown competing here is the ladies team from Cambridge VW Club.

racing. And although, in theory, you could drive your car to and from the circuit, you really need a dedicated race car plus trailer and tow car. Further details can be obtained from Big Boys' Toys Promotions.

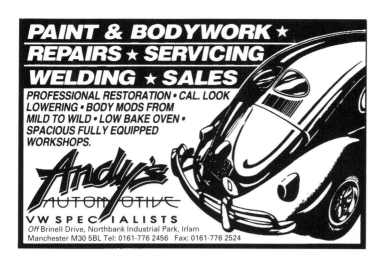
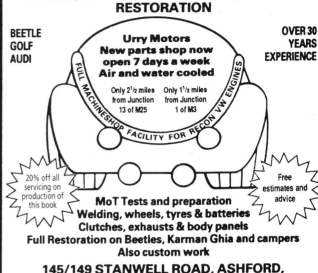

Rallying covers a wide range of activities, from navigational events which are not much more than treasure hunts, for which any everyday road car is suitable, up to full-blooded special stage rallies where you need an exceptionally strong and powerful car and all the mandatory safety equipment. VW clubs do not organise rallies beyond the 'treasure hunt' level; for the more serious rallies, you have to join a motor club recognised by the RAC Motor Sports Association.

VW Events

A great many get-togethers are organised for VW (mostly air-cooled) enthusiasts. Such events usually include a *concours d'elegance*, custom car show, autojumble sales and trade stands. Sadly, the best-known such event — VW Action, which was first staged in 1976 — was discontinued in 1994 due to difficulties in finding a suitable and cost-effective venue. VW Action provided camping facilities and attracted VW clubs from overseas. As well as a *concours d'elegance*, it featured driving competitions, gymkhana events such as a 'Bug-Push' and a timed engine-change contest.

Similar events, all well worth attending, include the British Volkswagen festival at Malvern, Worcestershire, in July; the Scottish VW Festival at Doune, Stirlingshire, in May; the Volkswagen Spring Festival near Maidstone, Kent, in April; the Stonor Park VW Festival in Buckinghamshire, in June; the Volksworld National Indoor Show at Sandown Park, Esher, Surrey, in March; and the Stanford Hall meeting in Leicestershire, in May.

VW drag race meetings at Avon Park Raceway and Santa Pod also have custom car shows and trade stands. *VW Motoring* and *Volksworld* magazines give details of all these events.

Any VW event, large or small, provides an invaluable opportunity to get together with like-minded people, to swap views and often to learn valuable lessons about driving, maintaining and enjoying the VW Beetle.

Unleaded Petrol

The official statement from Volkswagen on the use of unleaded petrol is that Beetles can be run on unleaded for four tankfuls out of five, i.e. that leaded petrol should be used every fifth tankful.

It is impossible, without stripping down the engine and checking the materials of its components, to say whether any particular Beetle can run exclusively on unleaded. The material which suffers without lead as a form of lubricant is cast iron. Any engine with cast-iron valve guides or cast-iron valve seats will have problems if it is run on unleaded fuel.

It is believed that all genuine Volkswagen factory cylinder heads since 1967 (at least for the American market) have hard chromed valve stems, bronze guides and steel valve seats, and these materials are perfectly satisfactory for operation on lead-free fuel. Current Mexican-produced Beetles are fitted with catalysts and therefore *must* be run exclusively on unleaded fuel.

Uncertainty arises when engines have been fitted with aftermarket replacement cylinder heads or valve guides. Some of the non-genuine heads are known to have cast-iron seats and guides. With these heads, or with genuine heads made before 1967, the sensible course is to avoid unleaded altogether.

Unless the engine has been radically modified, there is absolutely no problem, in the UK, with octane rating. In standard form, no Beetle has a compression ratio greater than 7.5 to 1 and the engine will run happily on 91 octane (or two-star,

Right and below: *There are plenty of opportunities for Beetle enthusiasts to purchase models and clothing depicting their favourite car.*

Above: Some Beetle drivers see themselves as being a breed apart from 'ordinary' motorists!

when it was available). Normal unleaded sold in the UK is 95 octane and there is nothing to be gained by using 'super plus'.

Do not be fooled into buying an 'unleaded' engine which simply has lower compression. If anything is needed to adapt a Beetle for unleaded, lower compression is certainly not it.

Below: The Beetle is well-known for its oversteering characteristic, which can be used to advantage in motorsport. Here Peter Noad, navigated by Sue Granger, gets SKT 328H well sideways on a special stage on South Bucks Motor Club's Rising Sun Rally.

If you check the valve clearances regularly, and at the same time check for any play between the valves and the guides, you can see if any wear is taking place through running on unleaded. If the valve clearances are closing, then the seats are wearing. Conversely, if the clearances remain constant you can continue to use unleaded with reasonable confidence.

Insurance

If your Beetle is worth more than a few hundred pounds, then it may be advisable to arrange insurance on an 'agreed value' basis. There are now many insurers who offer classic car agreed value cover. Photographs of the car are usually required, showing outside, interior and engine. In some cases, an engineer's inspection and valuation may be required. (Note: modified engines and customised Beetles may not be viewed very favourably in this context!)

For this type of insurance, there is usually a limit on annual mileage — possibly as little as 1,500 miles or as much as 7,500 miles — with premiums graded accordingly. There may be a requirement for the car to be kept in a locked garage. Details of classic car insurance can be obtained when you join the Volkswagen Owners Club or from companies who advertise regularly in *VW Motoring*, *Volksworld*, *Popular Classics* and elsewhere.

V.W. AUDI REPLACEMENT PARTS...
WE'VE GOT IT COVERED.

URO – the UK's leading independent supplier offers you:–
- The largest range of top quality products for VW/Audi vehicles available in the UK aftermarket*, including bodywork, engine, transmission and suspension.
- Over 100 owner operated outlets throughout the UK, each renowned for their specialist VW/Audi knowledge and their genuine interest in helping you maintain and improve your vehicle. So whatever you need before you go anywhere else check out your local URO outlet.

- URO buys from the same sources as the vehicle manufacturer where ever possible to ensure you get the best of Quality, Price and Service.
- All URO outlets are supported by a national network of computer linked distribution centres designed to get you the part you need with the absolute minimum of delay.
- Wake up to URO and keep your car in tip top condition, check our national advertising for details of your nearest outlet or contact the address below.

  * excluding VAG

...Wake up to-
URO
AUTOMOTIVE

URO Automotive, Unit 21, Fort Industrial Park, Dunlop Way, Birmingham B35 7AR.
Tel: 021 749 4700. Fax: 021 748 2198